THE
TIGER BAY
STORY

NEIL M. C. SINCLAIR, M.A.

THE
TIGER BAY
STORY

Copyright ©2003 Neil, M.C. Sinclair, M.A.

ISBN 0-9530859-0-2

The Tiger Bay Story was orignally published by Dragon & Tiger Enterprises in 1997 and previously published by BHAC in 1993.

Typeset by Marco Gil-Cervantes
Cover Design by Bev Morgans & Neil Sinclair
Printed by Zenith Media Gwasg Anterth

Published & Distributed by
Dragon & Tiger Enterprise
199 Loudoun Square, Cardiff Bay
Cardiff, CF10 5JJ, South Wales
Tel: (029) 2048 1129

DEDICATION

To the fond memory of my brother
Ronald W. Sinclair
(1937 - 1953)

ACKNOWLEDGEMENTS

Without the use of the facilities and staff at Fullemploy Wales, Coptic House in Mount Stuart Square, Cardiff, this work would not have been possible. Special thanks to Jackie Aplin, Acting Editor of Making Waves, for her suggestion that I submit my work to the Welsh Academy, to Suzanne Duval for her unending warmth and encouragement and to Lorenzo Del Gaudio for his contributions. To my sister, Leslie Clarke, who read parts of the early manuscript and encouraged me to continue. To Olwen Watkins, who once told me: "Don't complain to me! Write about it." And that is precisely what I did. I also thank Tony Bianchi of the Welsh Arts Council and Glenn Jordan and the staff of Butetown History & Arts Project. Further, I owe a debt of gratitude to Mrs. D. E. Bermingham for donating photographs taken by her late husband, D. P. F. Bermingham, who took the pictures of Tiger Bay during the demolition period while working as a staff officer at H.M.S. Cambria, a naval training establishment located in the docks. A special thank you must go to John Taylor, who devoted himself to processing and assisting in the organising of the photographs for this edition, and to everyone in the community who donated family snapshots to this project. Finally, to the community of Tiger Bay, I give my warmest thanks and appreciation and, ultimately, I give my thanks to the Holy Spirit for without them both I would not be who I am.

CONTENTS

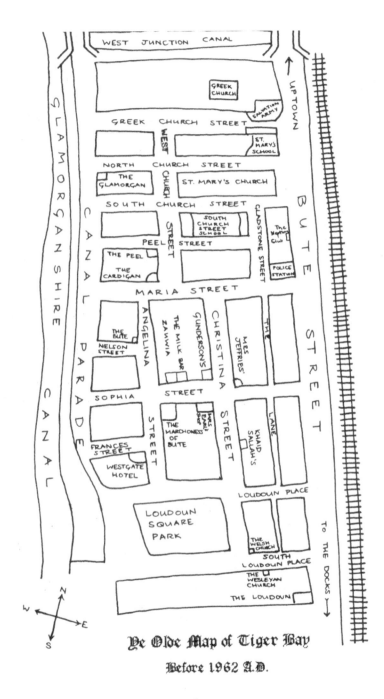

Ye Olde Map of Tiger Bay

Before 1962 A.D.

vi

INTRODUCTION FOR THIS EDITION

In the ten years since *The Tiger Bay Story* was first published, the local community has seen many changes to its surroundings. As a result of the environmental transformation of the area,undertaken by the Cardiff Bay Development Corporation, a great deal of academic research has been focused on Tiger Bay's remnant community and is one of the reasons this book is still in print. However, apart from typological errors which have been corrected here, one of its short-comings was the failure to include many stories I believed I had included in it, but which remained in mind only. Perhaps their omission was a blessing in disguise, because their absence led to the writing of *Endangered Tiger*, a companion volume to *The Tiger Bay Story*.

     Despite its success however, upon its initial publication, *The Tiger Bay Story* did stir passions among local residents, to say the least, prompting some like Peggy Farrugia to say so in print.

     "Where was the sense in what you wrote?" one of old Tiger Bay's respected and outspoken defenders fervently inquired in her letter to the October 1993 edition of *Making Waves*. In addition, Peggy Farrugia's communication to the magazine further proclaimed that:

> To write the only story about Tiger Bay would require a genius. Reading Neil's book was like being in Miss Ollie's front room trading stories. Strangers would believe it but for those who know, it was a load of rubbish. When, and if, I ever complete my *True* Tales of Tiger Bay, if people don't agree with it they can take it up with the folk I'll have got the stories from. We would all love to recapture the old days because they remind us of our youth, but ... those days are gone never to return. ... We all have to accept that the old way of life in old Tiger Bay has faded into the past. ... So Folks, let them write their stories. We know different, and words are only wind.

No one would disagree that words may only be wind but there are, of course, four of them. Clearly, to some my words blow in a different direction. That is why I wrote in the preface "if other works do exist in print of life in Tiger Bay written by authors from their personal observation, especially concerning the early days, I merely want mine to stand next to those works so that together the portrait of our community life is all the more enhanced."

Furthermore, many could benefit from *trading stories* in Miss Ollie's front room if this is, indeed, a reference to former teacher and life-time resident of Loudoun Square, Olwen Watkins née Blackman. Thus, I sincerely hope the *true tales* will eventually be written but I can not agree with the assertion that *The Tiger Bay Story* was "a load of rubbish." Nor, on the other hand, can I overlook the fact that it managed to offend and cause pain both to members of my own family and consequently myself.

In defense of *The Tiger Bay Story*, I am compelled to say that its contents were never consciously intended as a device to denigrate anyone. But, as its author, I take full responsibility for how I focussed on such a small portion of my step-grandmother's life. Written in response to defamatory remarks about old Tiger Bay that periodically appear in the media, short anecdotes, in contrast to well-balanced autobiographies, were the essence of that book. As indicated in its preface, I simply hoped that "no one will be offended by their inclusion or, as the case may be, exclusion." Reassuringly, although there is no disputing the obvious deterioration of the old community at the current time, I regard the passionate reaction to *The Tiger Bay Story* as a life affirming measure of the community's desire to preserve its ongoing existence.

Neil Sinclair
Tiger Bay
January 2003

PREFACE

"Mae hen 'wlad fy mamau yn annwyl i fi…"

This story is not much older than 150 years and began when Cardiff was a mere village near Caerphilly. Some time between that time and 1840, it was destined to become the "Saudi Arabia" of the 19th Century when the then Marquis of Bute chose to make it the world's major exporter of Black Gold: Coal. This City was the world's prime energy producer before oil succeeded it. Without the preceding event we, as a community, may never have existed,

And so this story is about a place. A place in Wales. I was born in that place. That place was Tiger Bay. But it should be made clear at the outset that this book is not about the author. If I knew any other way to tell it, I would do so. However, I know no other way to present this story that would capture the flavour and character of a community unique in the annals of British History.

As a youth in the Tiger Bay community of the 1940s and 1950s, I was entirely fascinated with the life of the people around me. What I witnessed I refer to such occurrences through my own personal experience. As to events before my time, of which I have no personal experience, these are recalled from the many moments spent at many a kitchen table or by a fireplace or nowadays in a pub or community centre imbibing the many tales passionately and humorously told of Old Tiger Bay from the people who knew them best. As such I hope that no one will be offended by their inclusion or, as the case may be, exclusion.

Over the years I considered writing this story as academically and historically as possible. However, many works that refer to Tiger Bay in this style already exist. For example, the opening chapter of "Negroes of Great Britain" by Kenneth Little and more recently Chapter 10 of Peter Fryer's "Staying Power" published in 1984. Both are quite complimentary reports but nothing of the humour and character of the day-to-day existence of life in Tiger Bay issues forth. However, given the context of the material surrounding them, these reports serve other purposes quite successfully.

Other historians have focused on "black coal" transported from Merthyr Tydfil and the valleys to the sea, or the subsequent "steel industry," as the subject of the general history of the growth of the Docklands. Here, the emphasis is on the intra-cultural richness and character of the contribution to the City of Cardiff made by the African, Middle Eastern and Asian heritage throughout this century. This heritage, intermingled with Maltese, Portuguese, Greek and other European nationalities, formed a multi-national society upon a Celtic Matrix that provided the basic ingredients that culminated in the birth of Tiger Bay.

Originally Tiger Bay was officially designated Bute Town in honour of the Marquis of Bute. Many of the street names — such as Maria (pronounced "Mariah"), Sophia, Frances, Angelina, Nelson, Patrick, Henry and Christina, to name merely a few — are alleged to be named after descendants and relatives of the same aforementioned Marquis.

On the other hand, the name Tiger Bay is representative of the community of people that emerged in Bute Town; and the origin of this name is steeped in many a myth. Of the many, there exist two versions that seem reasonable enough. One refers to an old song that was sung in the pubs and drinking halls frequented by seamen. The song contained a line that referred to Old Tiger Bay and, some say, this is how the name came about. The other was allegedly told by Portuguese seamen, who claimed that sailing into the rough waters, along the Severn Estuary into the bay leading into Cardiff Docks, was like sailing into "Una bahia de los tigres" — that is, into "a Bay of Tigers." Hence the name Tiger Bay.

Whatever the origin of the name, ever since the dawn of its people a negative mythology has surrounded it. Disparaging second-hand "hearsay" remarks — such as: "You couldn't walk down the streets (in safety) in Tiger Bay!" "It was dangerous there!" "Harm would come to you there!" "It was a terrible place. People gambled openly in the street!" etc. — can still be heard today from people who, on the whole, never set foot in Tiger Bay.

Clearly, the foregoing was mythological. People living their lives in Tiger Bay were never afraid to walk down any street. These were proud streets which displayed the obligatory semi-circular arms-length washing of the pavement by the housewives from the stoop in front of their homes; proud streets where, in any case, all doors were open, weather permitting, and rarely if ever locked!

In general most other articles and works on Tiger Bay are, to my knowledge, disparaging. Thus, no anthropological or sociological study will be found here. That has already been accomplished. No it is this, Tiger Bay from the inside out, that I want to bring to life in these pages. This I personally do not want to pass from the pages of history unrecorded. Yet, if other works do exist in print of life in Tiger Bay, written by authors from their personal observation, especially concerning the early days, I merely want mine to stand next to those works so that together the portrait of our community life is all the more enhanced.

Tiger Bay was actually a very tiny piece of earth. Much smaller than many realise even today, as can be seen from its description in Chapter Four, entitled "Up the Bay, Down the Docks." And the hand-drawn map at the beginning of this book will further express how small this piece of "terra firma" used to be.

This tiny piece of land. This "country" within the capital city of Wales, wherein emerged an Afro-Celtic culture admidst its intra-cultural and multi-ethnic heritage. This ground we love. This sacred territory which holds and held a utopian microcosm of social harmony dear to those who lived it — this is what I hope to have revealed within the pages of this little book. This Tiger Bay.

Chapter One

REMINISCENCES OF STREETS NO MORE

If my imagination took to the sky, I could almost see castles or even faces engaged in conversation in the formation of clouds above the narrow streets of Tiger Bay, when I was a child. It was the same with our fireplace. At home I used to sit in the "living room" in front of the fire, especially late in the evening after supper when it was getting dark. No television then! Our radio was situated on a shelf to the right of the fireplace above mother's armchair. It was a Rediffusion. Dad's easychair was opposite Mam's. I had a little stool placed between the two of them whilst we listened to the latest radio mystery. As a rule, the subject was too adult for me to comprehend so practically every night I would find myself drifting into the fire between the dark coals inside to a burning red hot interior. There, when my imagination took wing, I saw many wondrous things. Many nights witches flew from one castle of coal to another, sometimes leaving the impression of their faces embedded in the coals. What marvelous flights they took. Monsters and goblins appeared now and then as occasionally gas would seep from the coal and blue and yellow flames would hiss out. Now, beside this fireplace was a scuttle where the coal was kept. If it was empty and Mam was all comfy, she used to say, "Go on love, go get the coal for us," and although it was said in tenderness, it also meant, "Go get it!"

On cold winter nights I didn't enjoy "getting it," because the coal house was outside in the backyard. Sometimes Patsy Clark, "The Coal" of North Church Street, would drop his sack in the cupboard under the stairs, but most of the time the coal was outside, in the back, in the dog's house. Ruff, of course, lived inside with us! He shared his place by the fire with

1

Farrouk, our Persian cat. Anyway, I'd run out and shovel up the coal and rush back to my warm stool near the fire hoping to return to the same mystical land where the fire had taken me before. Unfortunately, the same path through the coals was impossible to rediscover. Nevertheless, with the magic of the fire and my innocent imagination, it wasn't hard to find a new place to explore.

Meanwhile, my parents would be still engrossed in the mystery which pervaded the living room by means of another magic: the wireless. While they were there, I would follow a beckoning friend into the warmth between the coals on into the glowing centre of the earth...

"You're not going to sleep again, are you, love?" Mam's voice would ring out.

"Why don't you go to bed?" Mam always had a way of giving orders while asking questions. And Dada had a way of finalising everything she said:

"Well, you heard your mother. Off you go then!" And sadly off I'd go, up the stairs, into my cold room and bed.

But some nights by the gaslight, the mantles of which were above the fireplace, Mam would tell me a story:

"It was a dark and stormy night and the captain said to his mate, 'Tell us a yarn, mate!' and the mate began, 'It was a dark and stormy night...'" I laughed as I jumped off my mother's knee when I first ever heard that recursive sea yarn.

Many nights a story would be told sitting by the fireplace in our little Victorian terraced house, one of 26 such houses in Old Frances Street — a street now gone some 30-odd years. 19 Frances Street was where I first became aware of the world and that world was the 1940s seaport community of the already legendary Tiger Bay, known to seamen everywhere.

Frances Street could be found sandwiched between Loudoun Square and Sophia Street with Old Angelina Street as an easterly boundary. At the other end, the old stone wall that ran the length of Canal Parade hid the Glamorganshire Canal from view. Victorian city planning had created quite a secluded haven from the rest of Tiger Bay for us "Frances Street Kids" in which to play.

Frances Street in the early 1950s with me on my first bicycle. Old Angelina Street is in the background.

Mrs Sharpes' — and subsequently Ghilan Farrah's — corner shop was number 1, opposite the Westgate Public House at the Old Angelina Street end. The rest of the street consisted of family homes and everyone on the street knew everyone else quite intimately. This goes without saying for the rest of Tiger Bay. Part of its uniqueness was this fact. We were the true definition of an "urban village." Everybody did know who your grandfather was, mother, relatives, etc. Which one was white, which "coloured." Which married Catholic, Moslem or Jew, and so on. There were the Williamses in number 2, Reggie, Ivor and "Googie" among them. In number 4 was Mrs Ali, who was white, like the Williams, but whose daughter Miriam was black, Somali to be exact, who, in turn, had a daughter named Lorraine. She and I were great friends. Opposite Joan Smith and her family resided the Limas, who were previously the Silvas, of number 21 — Johnnie, my best friend; his brother, Albee; and all their sisters, Valerie, Josie, Netta and Margie, to name only a few. As with most of the homes in Tiger Bay, the Limas' house was furnished with old Victorian furniture. I was always fascinated by the enormous dark wood table they had in their living room, practically taking up all the space they had. Something befitting the Knights of the Round Table, I thought.

At the moment, I will not belabour the reader with the names of all the families on Frances Street now. Many others will be finding their places in the pages of this story as it unfolds.

As I said, one end of Frances Street was flanked by old Angelina Street and I have to say something about this, because in a sense that part belonged to Frances Street too. Aunty Sarah Link, who was black, was always nice to us kids but she was just a little around the corner next to the "Gaucci's," who ran the "bookies." Aunty Sarah was not a relative but it was customary, at that time, for all the children in Tiger Bay to refer to older people of the community as Aunty or Uncle. It was also customary to call married women by their maiden name too. I suppose this reflects some sort of Tiger Bay tribal recognition. Anyway, though not very old, Aunty Sarah died of an illness that was only whispered about then: cancer.

Mr Shepherd lived with his family near Aunty Sarah for a time. He was my first impression of a communist blackman. He always carried his socialist newspapers under his arm and, although I was only a child with no sense to understand such politics, I did clearly understand that Mr Shepherd was obviously a man dedicated to the cause. He had two sons, Alan and Bobby, one of whom helped him with his paper delivery. I always remember him as that "nice Mr Shepherd." As a matter of fact, it was his television that was used in a marquee tent in

4

Loudoun Square Park so that everyone could see the Queen being crowned on Coronation Day. Mind you, some people say it was Eddie Gomez's television. I won't argue over that! Eddie later opened the Pineapple Club around 1956 at the top end of Canal Parade on the street of houses that faced the wall of the Great Western Railway, where Betty and Henry Kingston lived and "Lorne Lesley" — Irenie Spetti to us — was born.

Anyway, getting back to the Frances Street Kids, Anthony Evora, Johnnie Lima and Albee Lima, Terry Walli, Michael Harmon and I rushed across the park to get in the tent to see the Queen being crowned only to find all the grown-ups crowded in front. We could barely see the telly, it being so small. All I recall was a box with a bluish light coming from it as grown-ups shoved us back. After all, telly was new then. Hardly anyone had one. Mrs Percy of number 11 was the first to have one in Frances Street. She had it placed in the "front" room so anybody passing could see in and know she had one. But Mr Gatehouse was the first to have a car! And did he polish it every day?

Soon Aunty Sarah and Mr Shepherd had gone and the "Norths," who were white, moved in. As it was, in my time, Mrs North had remarried and Valerie, her beautiful daughter with long red hair, was raised by an Afghani stepfather. Then there were Michael and Gwennie, the children of Margie Harmon, also white, who definitely lived exactly opposite Frances Street.

Then there was Aunty Francis, Tiger Bay born of the Soaris (Suarez?) family, of Black Portuguese and Celtic heritage. I think her ancestry was Cape Verdean on the Portuguese side. She had Anthony and Phillipa and their house was dead centre to Frances Street and the front of their house used to be a shop of some sort. In there Anthony and I played among the remains of what was Mr Evora's workshop, much to the distraction of Dean-Dean, the old Cape Verde lodger, who used to chastise us. Anthony's father was an architect but he had been living in London since long before I could recall. Dean-Dean was a nice old black Portuguese man. He used to take Anthony and I to the "Bug House," as the Central Cinema on the Hayes was endearingly called. The Central Cinema used to change the pictures every few days but it was the serials — "Flash Gordon and the Clay People," "Rocket Man," etc. — that were a must for us. When Dean-Dean took us we didn't have to pay.

Next to them came Aunty Gladdie, whom I believe was also part Portuguese. She was nice but, being quite up there in age she mostly sat sedately in a chair by the front door and watched us. And right next door, slightly going out of Frances Street's view, lived another Silva family, not related to the ones on Frances Street but cousins to the Evoras. Christina was closer to my age but she also had older brothers. Among them Jon (Johnny Silva) was to become quite a well-known jazz vibraphonist years later.

Now, out of the previously described enclave, we kids formed a little Frances Street gang, a rainbow tribe that played together every day, weather permitting, under the watchful eye of the aforementioned adult folk.

Our game of "rounders" in the middle of the street might end abruptly as contact with the world at large would suddenly intervene. The sound of heavy footsteps, echoing along Canal Parade, accompanied by deep voices resounding out in unison:

We are the boys from Tiger Bay,
Ooh aah, ooh aah aah.
We are the Cardiff Boys.
We know our manners,
We spend our tanners,
We are respected wherever we go.
Marching down the old camp road,

Doors and windows open wide.
I tiddly i tie brown bread,
Ever seen a copper drop down dead?
We are the Cardiff Boys.

A gang of Nelson Street kids headed by Nick Parker, son of Victor Parker, would march by. The game would end and we would rush to join in procession with the others, singing at the top of our voices. It wouldn't be long before you would hear, from the direction in which we were heading, voices of another group, already marching in Loudoun Square:

We are the girls from Tiger Bay,
Ooh aah, ooh aah aah.
We are the Cardiff Girls.
Etc.

Then we would all end up playing Conkers, Gobs (often known elsewhere as "Jacks") or Allies, which were marbles to the rest of the world. Conkers fell off the conker trees in the park in Loudoun Square. They had a sort of chestnut inside which we used to pierce and put a string through. We'd then try to crack each others conkers with it.

Another game of which kids in Tiger Bay were fond was Rat Tat Ginger — the best way to annoy otherwise peaceful households. Members of the Frances Street Kids would be dared to knock someone's door and run away. But as this was Tiger Bay, you had to be ingenious. One night while hiding around the corner by the Westgate pub, Anthony Evora, Johnnie Lima and I tied a long string of wool on to Mrs Ali's door knocker in Frances Street and pulled. Anthony had taken the ball of wool from his mother's knitting basket under penalty of a severe thrashing with a cane from his mother should she ever find out! Anyway, in the darkly illumined gas lit street, old Mrs Ali didn't see the string when she came out. So we waited a goodly time for all to get comfortable and pulled again, all the while sniggering to our clever selves. Nothing happened. "Pull it again!" said Johnnie — and we pulled. Only someone seemed to be pulling the other end. As we peered around the corner, there was Miriam Ali, Mrs Ali's daughter, in all her fury. As she threatened to do us murder, we quickly scarpered down to our hiding place behind the park wall in Loudoun Square, thanking God for our close escape.

On another occasion behind the same wall, I was dared to knock Mrs Laferla's door. This Maltese family home was

Children playing in Old Loudoun Square (circa. 1950). Note the "Parkee's Hut" behind the little girl standing on the seesaw.

near the lamppost on the north side of Loudoun Square, near the "Parkee's Hut," as we called the little house the park-keeper stayed in during the day. Well, with the lamplight shining on to the door, pulling this family's knocker was a dangerous enterprise. On the other hand, the Laferlas had a great elaborate knocker which was hard to resist. So, reluctantly, I crept over the wall and up to the door, then knocked and ran for cover. Alas, nothing happened and I was dared to go do it again. So, over the wall I crept. Just as I was lifting the knocker, the door flung open and there was Mrs Laferla in her pinafore, sweeping broom in hand! I fled back across the street and over the wall: the others were already running across the park for their lives. Here comes Mrs Laferla, scaling the park wall, running behind us all the while swinging the broom in the air. Our youth outran the old dear but the broom only missed us by inches when she was flinging it. But more of this later, as it is too soon to venture far away from Frances Street.

My father, Walter Sinclair, being a bosun, was away quite a lot in my early years and my first impression of him seems to be his return home with his seaman's kit-bag stacked high on the living room floor. Out of this kit-bag came my first ever clockwork train set. It had been made in Russia. Little did I comprehend, in those days, that my dad had been in captivity in Vladivostok towards the close of World War II. But then seamen were always away from home, so a seaman's absence was a natural part of family life. I remember also that time I had a child's toy post office set and with the mocky stationery decided to write to Dad when he was at sea. On the envelope I put a teddy bear stamp and while out with my Mam, who was shopping, I actually popped it into the red and black pillar box. Well, that letter actually arrived at its destination much to the joy and amazement of the captain and crew. My father kept it throughout his entire life.

My father was born in 1910 in Peel Street. He came from

a large family and 37 Peel Street remained the family home until Peel Street, like Frances Street, was no more, some time back in the early sixties.

Walter Sinclair, bosun on board the SS Trevelyan with Malay seamen.

My father's mother was Helen Margaret Lewis, who had a sister name Elizabeth. Their family originally came from somewhere in or near Chepstow and settled in Cardiff prior to the turn of the century. These Celtic matriarchs were to become the founders of two of old Tiger Bay Afro-Celtic families still extant.

Until the immigration influx of the 1950s changed the British social complexion, the contribution to South Wales from the Third World consisted almost totally of males — seamen. Those who got married here usually married Celtic and Anglo-Saxon brides. During the 1950s, Third World women also came, bringing and maintaining their home cultures on British soil. But this was not the case at the turn of the century when Welsh women were the heads of the households of Third World men.

Three members of the Lewis family and friends at the turn of the 20th century. Back row left is: Auntie Betty with sister, Helen Margaret, next to her. Brother, Jimmy, who died in the Battle of Jutland, front centre. The Afro-Celtic child on his lap was a neighbour's child.

Helen Margaret, my grandmother, married Danny Sinclair, who as a young lad, before the turn of the century, left the torrid Caribbean climate of his home in Christchurch, Barbados, where he was born in 1879. As a cabin boy of 15 years, he decided to jump ship in Bristol, leaving behind the hardship of a seaman's life. British Colonial plantation life was also now behind him. He quickly made his way to Tiger Bay, where he believed he would be welcome and so began the Sinclair family. At about the same time, his cousin, Walter St Clair, after whom my father is named, arrived. And both the St Clair and Sinclair families are to be found in Butetown or in or near Cardiff to this very day.

Clearly, Danny must have spent some time in Italy before coming to Wales, because it has been said that he spoke fluent Italian. Anyway, in Cardiff, apart from the sea, little work was obtainable for a "coloured man" at that time. Nevertheless, Danny managed to get a horse and cart and even got cited for speeding somewhere along Newport Road!

By 1913, Helen Margaret had given birth to Leslie, George, Walter and Christian, the only girl at that time. To make ends meet, when he wasn't at sea, Danny began to run a  gambling house in Peel Street. More children were to come when he married Mary Ann Jones of Cardiff after the premature death of Helen Margaret. Tommy, Billy, Sarah, Cleo, Helen and Jackie were to make their presence felt in Tiger Bay in the time to come. Despite his going to sea, keeping a gambling house and maintaining a large family, Danny Sinclair still had time to be Captain of the Coloured International Cricket Club during the mid-1920s.

My grandmother, Helen Margaret Sinclair, Welsh wife of Danny Sinclair.

At the same time as these events were occurring, Aunty Betty, my grandmother's sister, Elizabeth, had married Alec James from St Lucia and soon there was another Alec, Henrietta and a Maggie among others. They, too, lived in Peel Street, number 13 to be exact. Their house was on the side nearest Canal Parade, next door but one to Betty Johnson, now Mrs Betty Campbell, who is currently Head Teacher of Mount Stuart Primary School in Butetown. Number 37, my grandfather's home, was opposite one of the back doors of the school yard of South Church Street School.

Imagine the thrill of the Board School pupils fleeing to freedom in front of your doorstep everyday!

When Maggie was still quite young, Danny's gambling house was going strong. She remembers that in the front room

Captain of the Coloured International Cricket Club, William Alonzo MacDonald Sinclair, otherwise known as "Danny" (front centre). Taken in the early 1920s in Loudoun Square Park.

there was a beautiful sideboard with a huge oval mirror on top of it. One day, when no one was around, she peeked inside the two drawers in the sideboard. In the first she saw paper money, lots of it. In the other, guns, knives, watches and jewellery — all pawned waiting to be reclaimed by sailors away at sea. She also recalls that Helen Margaret could handle any trouble if any of the gamblers got out of line. That old Celtic temper could be put to good use when needed.

Around 1922, the Headleys had moved into 19 Frances Streeet when Beatrice, who was soon to grow up and marry my father, was about 13 years old. She was a quiet and exceedingly shy young girl, who soon became entranced with all the goings on in Tiger Bay. At the drop of a hat, there was always a celebration or "do" taking place that caused the local musicians to get together. Every household utensil would be used as well as mandolins, guitars, pipes and bones to bring Calypso music to life, the melodies drifting rhythmically out above the slate-tiled roofs and chimneys of the little terraced houses of Tiger Bay, beyond to the hills and valleys and the green, green grass of the ancient land of Morgan.

At a Christening or wedding or even a funeral, events that lasted several days, Beatrice was fascinated by men with names like "Bengal Tiger," "One Armed Joe," "Hand In Pocket," and "King of Beasts" (who Maggie eventually married) and so many more local characters, who danced and entertained everyone on these occasions. On Christmas and New Year's Eve, front doors opened wide at night-time to let the roving troubadours in.

Of all the guitar players, George Glossop from St Vincent was apparently one of the best. That was one of the reasons Victor Parker used to travel over to Roath to get George to "learn" him to play. Victor was nearly 20 before he finally consented to teach him. George's daughter, Laura, fondly remembers watching her father standing behind Victor, holding his fingers in place instructing him in how to make the proper chords.

Besides Laura, George Glossop was father to Evelyn, Charlotte and Mary, who became the mother of Mary and Redvers Sango of Hodges Row. (As it is, Hodges Row has been replaced by Hodges Square nowadays.) There was also Bill, Charlie and George-the-younger, who like his father was an excellent classical guitar player. As a matter of fact, George-the-younger was referred to as the second "Django Reinhardt" so the rumours of the quality of his playing must be true. He teamed up with Stanley Dodd and travelled to London taking Victor with them to do a very popular show that had a South Sea Island flavour.

Unfortunately, George-the-younger had to take his music to war. The mechant ship he sailed on was torpedoed by the German fleet early in World War II. All the black merchant seamen, along with the rest of the British crew, were taken on board the invincible "Bismarck" as captives (Carlos de Pas, our local artist, was among them.) But George still had his guitar with him and his music made the war-time days seem bright, even for the German captors. When the Allies attacked the Bismarck, George and the rest of his unfortunate companions were still on board and all had to find a safe haven. George even helped some of his German captors to safety and gave assistance to the wounded German soldiers.

Victor Parker, well known musician and entertainer and favourite of Old Tiger Bay.

Nevertheless, they were taken to a prison camp in Germany. Out came the guitar again. George's music proved very popular, even with the German officers. Tragically, he suffered from severe headaches for which he underwent two operations in Germany. He subsequently died there of a brain haemorrhage, leaving his brother Bill to continue the guitar playing tradition at home.

Victor Parker went on to follow in George Glossop's footsteps and became a well known jazz musician and favourite of Tiger Bay. Although he stammered painfully when speaking, remarkably when he sang it was with perfect diction. In the 1950s and 1960s, he often played at the Quebec pub, which was located on the corner of Hope and Crichton Streets, not far from the Custom House pub in Bute Street.

As I mentioned earlier, closer to the turn of the century,

Aunty Betty was born, lived and died in Peel Street, although her father originated somewhere near Chepstow. Aunty Betty, my paternal grandmother's sister, married Alec James, who came to Tiger Bay from St Lucia at the age of 18. When I talked with her as I prepared this book, Maggie reminisced about her mother's four brothers, Uncle Neppie, Danny, Dada Willie, and Jimmy — all of them Lewises. During the Great War, one of the brothers died of malaria in Mesopotamia and Jimmy died on a ship during the Battle of Jutland. The other two died soon after. So Aunty Betty lost all her brothers while she was quite young.

On the left, Auntie Betty with her daughters: Maggie and Henrietta with Billy Neil, Henrietta's son, sitting on Maggie's lap. Taken in the early 1930s on a visit to Tenby, where Maggie was working in service.

During this time, Aunty Betty also had an uncle who had been in the Welsh Guards. After his military stint, Uncle Levi kept a blacksmith shop on the River Taff, near Blackweir, and from there he made regular weekend visits to his relatives in Tiger Bay. He downed many a pint at the Peel, the pub on the corner at West Church Street. However, there came a time when he did not come and the family wondered what had happened to him until Aunty Betty saw his photograph in the *South Wales News* with a report that said he had fallen into the Glamorganshire Canal and drowned.

Maggie had two sisters, Henrietta and Helen. She also had a brother, Kipper, whose real name was Billie. He liked playing rugby and was muscial too. He taught himself to play guitar and played with Victor Parker and someone else who could play the mandolin. Now Kipper had a soft heart for a lady down the street named Rosie Condon, who liked a drink or two. So, if Kipper didn't come home, everyone knew he was down Rosies. However, due to a rugby injury, he took ill and was convalescing in the front room. Unfortunately, on a night that turned out to be very cold, Kipper caught pneumonia and later died.

Later, Maggie had a brother named Alec. Poor Alec also took ill and was taken to St David's Hospital. In those days, you weren't allowed to see children in hospital. Anyway, as there seemed no hope for Alec, Aunty Betty wanted him home to die in Peel Street. These were very poor times and Aunty Betty had to go to the Maria Street Police Station and ask Gerry Brobin, a people's policeman, to help her get transport to have Alec brought home. An ambulance was more than she could afford. Alec spent his last few days in that same front room as Kipper and died in the late afternoon. Someone in the community recalls that, as his funeral cortege left the house, an offical figure was seen to arrive in Peel Street asking for the few shillings owed for his stay in hospital.

Coming home from the cemetery, Aunty Betty asked Maggie where her father was, as no one had seen him. When they got home, Maggie went upstairs and found her father sitting on his son's bed, holding a photograph of Alec in his hand, sobbing.

That night, while Maggie slept upstairs in 13 Peel Street, she felt an extremely cold chill. She awoke in the middle of the night and called out to her father.

"What time is it?"

"Two o'clock," he said.

The next day, Maggie's father asked her what was going on during the night. She said he would only laugh at her. But he said no, he thought he understood. So she told him she saw Alec in her bedroom and her father said:

"I know he came to me and looked over my bed but Kipper came and put his arms around him and took him away."

Maggie was afraid but her father said not to be afraid of these things. He was somewhat into the Obeah of the West Indies and understood these spritual things.

In my childhood, when I used to visit my relatives in Peel Street, I always found Aunty Betty seated on a chair by her front door, usually surrounded by her family. She always used to invite me to sit upon her lap. I felt protected in her strong arms and while there, like her, watched the world go by. Henrietta, Aunty Betty's daughter, and her daughter, who was also called Betty, were close by, as were my cousins Lesley Neil and Sandra Cockle. I can still see her, Aunty Betty, a matriarch with her great nephew upon her lap completely encircled by her brown-skinned offspring. In retrospect, I suppose some would consider it odd that I didn't realise that my Aunty Betty was a white lady until I was many years older. It seems distinctions based on skin colour did not bear any significance in our lives in those times.

Meanwhile, across the street at number 37, as was said earlier, Helen Margaret died and Danny, who would later be my grandfather, married Mary Ann Jones, who was only sixteen years old at the time. Of Danny and Helen Maragaret's four children George and Leslie also died, which left Walter, the eldest, and Christian to be raised by Mary Ann.

Life on Peel Street with a stepmother was to change things, as Christian soon discovered. Mary Ann's love of horse racing may have had a lot to do with it. While Danny was at sea, to makes ends meet, the household furniture and furnishings were taken to the pawnshop in Bute Street and Christian and her older brother made do with the bare necessities. Now, Mary Ann wasn't daft: she occasionally scanned the newspaper to see when Danny's ship was due to return — that is, when she wasn't indulging in her favourite pastime, studying which horse to back. Once news of Danny's ship's return was published, all the furniture would be dragged or "horse and buggied" back to 37 Peel Street.

Danny never seemed to believe his children's stories of the furniture being taken away while he was gone, but he always lent an ear when Mary Ann complained that Christian was getting out of control. Christian always believed that her stepmother didn't like her because she reminded her of her mother, Margaret Helen, whose likeness was so striking in her face.

On one of her mean spirited days, Mary Ann told Danny that his daughter was too much to handle and she was seeing far too many boyfriends. She added that she strongly suspected that "Chrissy," as she was being called by then, was having a baby! Being a man of his times, Danny knew this would bring disgrace to the family, so he agreed with Mary Ann's decision to have her sent away.

Chrissy was 13 when she was told she was being sent to a convent somewhere on the other side of Chepstow. Walter, her brother, who had by now married, was told to escort her in the hired horse and carriage [in reality it was an early motor car and a priest also accompanied them] that was to take her away from Tiger Bay forever. His wife, Beatrice, went with them.

Of course, no one was permitted to mention why Chrissy was being taken away and, besides, in those very Victorian days, you couldn't even whisper the subject. So her brother and sister-in-law sat silently as she was transported away to the nuns. For many years after, she resented her brother for this, although, at that time, he didn't know why she had to be sent away.

Despite her bitter pain, Chrissy found a degree of happiness with the nuns, who treated her kindly. Mind you, she had to do her chores! But, as time went by, the nuns became alarmed with the realisation that Chrissy was not with child and immediately sent word to her father that this was the case. With this news, Danny immediately stopped sending the shilling a week he had to pay for her keep. As a result of this action, the nuns told Chrissy she would have to go back home because her father was no longer paying her board and lodging. However, Chrissy protested. She was never going back there! So she determined to go to London.

Christian Sinclair ("Chrissy") in the 1930s.

Now, the employment prospects for a coloured girl in the difficult times of the late 1920s and early 1930s were not bright. If she was blessed with talent, she could, however, find work in the show business night life of London's West End, in and around the streets of Soho, near Piccadilly. Chrissy danced as a chorus girl in these clubs and spent much of her free time around the excitement generated by "Hutch," a black band leader quite popular in London in those days. As part of London's night life "exotica," she even got a bit part in the movie "Cleopatra," which was being made then. Of course, when news of Chrissy's showbiz career reached Tiger Bay, Danny became enraged. Good women were never seen on the stage in those days! Nevertheless, her sisters and brothers often came up to London to stay with her, keeping her in touch with life in Tiger Bay.

While working in a pub in Old Compton Street in Soho, Chrissy got a part in an all "Negro" American dance show and did very well with them. Even though World War II was rapidly approaching, this troupe was invited to appear in Paris.

Chrissy was overwhelmed with excitement. There was the possibility of fame. But there was a snag: she needed a passport. That meant going to Tiger Bay because, as she was not 21 yet, Danny would have to sign her papers.

Needless to say, when Chrissy arrived at the Peel Street home, Danny refused to give his approval. So she spent some time with her brothers and sisters, who had been growing up while she was away. It was about this time that her father died.

Chrissy, sadly, went back to her life in London and the war raged on. She soon discovered that the dance troupe that had gone to Paris had been taken by the Nazis and were never heard from again. One up for Danny, she thought retrospectively.

Of course, with the war the Yanks were in town and it wasn't long before her "Negro" American soldier boy was to sweep her off her feet and Henry Kennard was to take his Afro-Celtic Welsh bride to his home in Boston, Massachusetts.

Chrissy was among the first war brides to make the transatlantic crossing. On board the passenger vessel at Southampton was a military band, a ship load of people and the excitement of brides off to new lives. Of course, they sang. "Play Jerusalem!" she shouted. And they obliged. "Jerusalem, Jerusalem, etc." "No, no," she exclaimed, "Not that one!" Then she sang, "And did those feet in ancient times..." — and all the British brides joined in. With Chrissy singing "Mae hen 'wlad fy nhadau" the ship departed. Chrissy wasn't to see Tiger Bay again until 1958.

As it does, life went on in Tiger Bay in Chrissy's absence and Mary Ann mellowed with age, although she remained somewhat cantankerous throughout her lifetime. When the spirit moved her, she would go on her rounds and visit the families of her children, as they created families of their own. One day, she decided on visiting her stepson, Walter, in Frances Street. Finding the front door wide open, she sat herself down in the living room, waiting for someone to come and receive her. She sat and sat for quite some time before she realised she was sitting in Noni Cameron's living room next door in number 18!

Well, the journey has begun and the flavour of old Tiger Bay is beginning to rise like the aroma of a well-cooked Sunday dinner. We have taken a trip along streets that exist no more and visited Old Loudoun Square, the centre of community activity.

A winters day in Old Loudoun Square. Late 1950s.

Of course, there is more to come. In the distance echoing in the still night air, standing there in Old Loudoun Square, one might hear the night piercing voice of Phonesine L'Aventure, strolling home from a night out with Mattie Kelly, singing the lilting strains of "Tiger Bay-ee, Tiger Bay-ee," and laughter as the merriment of the night out gradually faded. Another voice, probably disturbed by the night sounds, bellows out:

"Don't forget to put out the ashes!"

After all, the following day the dustmen will be coming

to take away the rubbish of the previous days — the ashes collected from all the coal-burning fireplaces lit on many a cold morning.

By the time I had grown up, the song "Tiger Bay-ee" was winding down from the days when it was sung with more flourish and gusto. But, at any special gathering of the Tiger Bay Clan, one could still hear the complete refrain:

Tiger Bay-ee, Tiger Bay-ee,
It's not very far from the Docks.
When you get to Loudoun Square,
Turn to your right and you are there.

Tiger Bay-ee, Tiger Bay-ee,
It's just like a fancy dress ball.
And if anyone can say,
They ain't been down the Bay,
Then they haven't seen Cardiff at all.

Chapter Two

WHEN LILAC AND JASMINE
GREW IN TIGER BAY

The one good thing about having your own home was having a garden out back. Mother loved to keep the garden with flowers — primroses, gladiolas, marigolds, sometimes daffodils and pansies. She also liked to grow vegetables. Grandfather had kept chickens in the back years before, so the soil was very fertile on either side of the garden path. Mother grew runner beans, tomatoes and potatoes. But the memory I recall best was the lilac tree that had grown in such a way as to hide the out door lavatory at the end of our garden. It had several trunks that permitted a small pathway up into the tree, where I loved to play as a child in the 1950s. But, what really put the finishing touches to our garden was the jasmine bush that belonged to Mrs MacDonald, the always old, white haired, Scottish lady, who lived next door in number 20, we called "Mrs Mac."

For years, the family waited for that jasmine bush to grow over the roof of our toilet — which it did when I was quite young. The aroma of lilac and jasmine have remained with me ever since and any where in the world where I smell them I am transported back to that little garden in Tiger Bay.

In a sense, we had a cosy little home complete with Mam and Dad, two brothers and a sister. Always a dog call Ruff and a Persian cat named "Farrouk." But for Mam arriving at 19 Frances Street, from her early beginnings at the turn of the century on Peel Street, to the time of my idyllic remembrances, was a long and sometimes bitter road to travel.

My mother's mother was Agnes Jolly, a Lancashire lass from Bamber Bridge, near Whitley Woods and Chorley. Agnes,

Ruff, mother and me in the backyard of 19 Frances Street in Old Tiger Bay during the 1940s.

whose childhood began prior to the turn of the century, was the last child of a large family, born during difficult times when not much money could be made working all day in the cotton mills. As a result, her family was forced into the dreadful decision to put her into Nazareth House. This institution was a home for orphans or children of overburdened families. For eight years, life for Agnes was movement from one home to another until the early 1900s, when she came to Penylan Convent in Cardiff, another home under the auspices of Nazareth House. There she met Maggie, a strictly Victorian-raised Cardiff girl, who when opportunity struck escaped the endless drudgery of laundry work in the convent and made her way down to the freedom one could find in the community of Tiger Bay.

It was through her acquaintance with Maggie that Agnes learned all about life in Tiger Bay. Meanwhile, in the Bay, as a result of her stern upbringing, Maggie became known as "Straight Jane And No Nonesense." Nonetheless, she became wife to Joseph Friday, a huge black man known as "Pop Friday," who originally came from Guyana, South America. In those days, it was British Guiana. They eventually settled down at 5 Somerset Street in Grangetown with dreams of living

Agnes Headley (née Jolly), wife of James Augustus Headley (circa 1910).

happily ever after. After all, World War I had yet to begin.

Having followed "Straight Jane And No Nonesense" down to Tiger Bay, Agnes soon met up with one of Pop Friday's seagoing friends, "Iron Ford." This handsome young man clearly swept Agnes off her feet for they, too, were soon to be married. Iron Ford, of course, was not his real name. He was James Augustus Headley. Like my grandfather, Danny Sinclair, known in Tiger Bay as "Gravy Eye," Iron Ford came from Barbados. Bridgetown to be exact. But not just a touch of the Ashanti was he. Carib blood was in his veins too. His ambition, like Gravy Eye's, was to escape sugar plantation life and head for Queen Victoria's land. But, as a lad, he was disembarked from his ship in Cuba. There he worked as a trolley car driver. One fateful day, he had the misfortune to run over a man in a Havana Street and thought he had killed him. In panic, he boarded a ship as soon as was possible, signing on as "Joe Ford," His job was cabin boy. Then destiny brought him to Wales, where his first view of life in Britain was in Tiger Bay.

Said to be mean-tempered and stern, characteristics that well earned him the name Iron Ford, he still softened enough at the sight of Agnes, whom he married and who subsequently gave birth to Beatrice, my mother, while living in lodgings in

James Augustus Headley, alias "Iron Joe Ford," husband of Agnes Headley (circa 1910).

Peel Street. And of that street old Mrs Pervoe was midwife to my mother's birth.

As no land work was available to black men in those times, Pop Friday and Iron Ford had to make many seagoing ventures to make ends meet. Eventually, Iron Ford was able to get lodgings for his family in Grangetown at 27 Somerset Street, near Pop and "Nana Friday," as Straight Jane And No Nonsense had, by then, become known.

Now war began to ravage Europe and by this time Iron Ford had discovered that the man he thought he had killed was very much alive in Cuba. So he could be James Augustus Headley once again. Unfortunately, "Iron Ford," as a nickname, had stuck and he was known as "Fordie" ever since.

Despite the war, James Augustus still went to sea. And while at sea, as a merchant seaman aboard a British ship, in the heat of battle, the Germans torpedoed his vessel three times. James was taken prisioner and placed in shackles aboard a German ship. It was indeed fortunate for him that this war was fought before the "pure race" philosophy had come to power as he never complained of mistreatment by the Germans and always spoke of the German soldier, who used to give him his

own dinner throughout the entire ordeal. When he did finally
return home, he had earned two bronze medals for his bravery
in service to the King.

By the time the war wound down, James was home and,
even though many of the multi-ethnic merchant seamen from
Tiger Bay had become landlubbers, he remained a seaman.

While many of the young British men had been away
fighting the war, circumstances had made it necessary to hire
women and whomever, regardless of race, in an effort to keep
industry going while the war raged. This, of course, did not
please the returning white war veterans who, even in those hard
working days of heavy industry, were unable to find decent
jobs in the post-war period.

Social dissatisfaction and tension was set to explode, as
seemed to be the situation in previous post-war periods throughout history. There had never been a war of such magnitude as
The Great War, hence the post-war situation was bound to be
particularly explosive. Instead of protesting at governmental
administrative ineptitude, social anxiety exploded in the form
of race riots in the United States and Great Britain. For
discontented whites the 1919 Riots were incited by the sight of
black men working, black men being easy victims of such
misguided anger. And despite its legendary social consciousness, South Wales was not exempt from this scourge as trouble
reared its head in Newport, Cardiff and Barry.

Killing and burning appeared in the streets of Cardiff and
were soon to arrive at Somerseet Street in Grangetown.

At that time, Beatrice was ten and had just celebrated a
party with all the neighbouring children, who, unlike her, were
white. They had all gone home after thoroughly enjoying
themselves, having consumed jelly and blancmange and the
like. Then, quite suddenly, chaos! A neighbour excitedly
appeared at the front door shouting, "They're on their way! Get
him out or they'll kill him!" Agnes ran with James to the back

door encouraging him to flee over the back wall to safety else he should die or be beaten senseless if the rioters found him in the house. As James fled, Agnes took Beatrice by the hand and rushed upstairs to the landing. Beatrice knew nothing of the "whys and wherefors" of all this commotion and was more confused than terrified as she hid away among the folds of the skirt of her mother's long, dark, floor-length dress. Sombre clothes were customary in those days. They did not know what happened at Pop and Nana Fridays across the street, but out of the many voices roaring in the street one was heard to say:

"Not here! Next door!"

Light from a flashlight could be seen through the glass window of the front door as Beatrice and her mother peered down from the landing. Suddenly, a few thuds and the door was broken through. While men ran into the downstairs rooms, Beatrice, in her fear, implored her mother to hide themselves under the bed, the safest place in the world in the mind of a child. But it wasn't them that the rioters wanted. Iron Ford, who had already escaped, was their prey.

Disappointed at not finding him, they began to ransack and destroy the home. Agnes was attacked and struck to the floor while the rioters poured paraffin over the living room table about to set fire to the house.

"Better not!" a voice blurted out.

"It's not their house!"

With that they left.

Holding on to each other in fear was the only consolation for mother and daughter as they awaited the arrival of a constable. The police arrived the following day and, for all her troubles, Agnes was blamed for marrying a black man! Beatrice was now keenly aware that she was "coloured" and needed to know what this was all about. Her mother, however, was too stunned to console her, being unable to get over the loss of her cosy little home. It was not long before a visit was paid by the landlord, who demanded that they leave or he would evict them. He wasn't having his property nearly burnt down on account of any black man. So into the streets they went....

In Tiger Bay, things were different. The "Bayites" were armed to the teeth. Chinese restauranteurs provided "plently pepper" to the housewives, pepper which was hurled into the faces of the horses on which the white rioters rode down into Bute Street. As the horses reared up and the white men fell, Tiger Bay men and women, boys and girls of every race and nationality you can think of pounced upon them and gave them the hiding they never forgot. Legend still proclaims Tiger Bay as a dangerous place to go!

No, there were no easy or defenseless victims to be had here. Tiger Bay was a fortress. In the days to follow, police manned the two bridges that were the northern entrances to Tiger Bay — the one at the top end of Bute Street and the one at the top of Canal Parade. Both bridges spanned the West Junction Canal. As the white rioters approached the bridges on horseback, they were told by the police that if they "went down there" they entered at their own risk because "They are ready for you down in the Bay." There were a few West African, West Indian, Arab and Somali families living in Herbert Street and the surrounding areas, just outside the protective enclave of Tiger Bay proper. They, however, did not fair so well.

Tiger Bay was the safest haven in Britain for men of colour. The people of Tiger Bay fought well for this tiny piece of land, for their communitys' right to be. Our Celtic [and Afro-Celtic] mothers fought in this battle too and preserved a harmonious multi-racial way of life, which forms one of the most endearing aspects of community life in the history of South Wales. In honour of that early valiant struggle this battle should rightfully be referred to as the "First War of Tiger Bay" to commemorate the community's keen spirit of togetherness. The legend of the knife-carrying inhabitants of Tiger Bay may have its root here in the need for self defense against a violent and hostile host nation.

In Chapter 10 of Staying Power: The History of Black People in Britain, in a section entitled "Under Attack," Peter Fryer captures the mood and momentum of this time to such a degree that I am compelled to quote him at length:

> As crowds gathered again that evening in St Mary Street, Custom House Street, The Hayes, and the top end of Bute Road, the black citizens of 'Loudoun Square, Maria Street, Sophia Street, and Angelina Street had established quietly determined means of self-protection.' They posted sentries, loaded their guns, and left no one in doubt of their mood, as a South Wales News reporter who got through the police cordon testified:
>
> > The coloured men, while calm and collected, were well prepared for any attack, and had the mob from the city broken through the police cordon there would have been bloodshed on a big scale, and the attacking force would have suffered heavily.... Hundreds of negroes were collected, but these were very peaceful, and were amicably discussing the situation among themselves. Nevertheless, they were in a determined mood, and ready to defend 'our quarter of the city' at all costs. They had posted sentries at each entrance to give notice of the approach of any hostile crowd.... An old resident of Loudoun-square told me that he and his wife had watched the negroes loading revolvers. They made no secret of it.... As my informant put it, 'There is enough arms and ammunition among them to stock an arsenal.' Long-term black residents said: 'It will be hell let loose... if the mob comes into our streets.... If we are unprotected from hooligan rioters who can blame us for trying to protect ourselves?'..."[1]

As a result of the success in defending itself from hostile attack, Tiger Bay became a Mecca for the Black, Arab, Malay and Chinese families in Cardiff. It was for this reason that James Augustus Headley had determined he would go back to sea and save enough money to buy a house down in Tiger Bay and dare any man to walk over his threshold uninvited.

However, while James was away, Agnes and Beatrice found themselves lodging in a Salvation Army hostel. When he was home from sea, they rented lodgings from friends of his but, given his short temper, this meant moving quite frequently. Nevertheless, in time James had saved enough money to consider buying his own home. At that time, the Erskine family of Old Angelina Street owned a row of houses on the south side of Frances Street and were willing to sell one to him. When he signed the final papers with the Erskines, James Augustus Headley became the proud owner of a continuing 99 year leasehold at 19 Frances Street.

At 13 years of age, his daughter Beatrice had come to know that the majestic refrain of "Land of Hope and Glory" somehow had nought to do with her. In the security that Tiger Bay could provide for its inhabitants, Beatrice was able to grow up unmolested by the racial anitpathy of the outside world. She did, however, have to endure the watchful and everpresent eye of a very strict father, who kept all possible suitors at bay from his very lovely, attractive, young daughter.

Anyway, once Beatrice had become attached to Walter Sinclair, who had also been her childhood friend in her early Peel Street days, she was never very interested in the older men, who dared to risk the wrath of Iron Ford. This couple, Beatrice and Walter, was destined to be together. Besides, her parents were becoming old and weary at an age that today we would consider quite young.

It was customary in those times for homeowners to take in lodgers and so Iron Ford rented a room to Twist, a young

Walter Sinclair, my father in his prime.

West Indian seaman. Iron Ford was very fond of this young man and treated him like the son, which Beatrice always felt her father wanted instead of her.

In a fit of rebellion against her father's continuing restrictions, Beatrice decided to run away to Penylan Convent. From the many stories her mother had told her about the nuns, Beatrice always regarded that convent as a place of refuge. So one day she got off the tramcar she took from Bute Street and walked through the open doors of the convent. At the close of the day, when the convent doors were locked, Beatrice was mistaken for one of the many orphans already residing there and, much to her chagrin, she fell under the strict supervision of the Mother Superior.

Her rude awakening came about when Beatrice discovered that the nuns weren't any less strict than her father and were not like her mother had led her to believe. She was soon given duties in the laundry room and made to do many difficult tasks. She also had to wear a uniform and what she thought was a silly hat.

It wasn't long before Beatrice felt homesick and wanted to leave. However, she wasn't permitted to do so, no matter how much she remonstrated about having parents. They seemed not to believe her. So she demanded to see the Mother Superior but never gained permission. What was she to do! she pondered.

Well, the day came when the opportunity arose. Beatrice

was scrubbing floors with another girl when from the heat of her brow she pulled her hat off her head.

"You've got to keep that on!" her companion warned her.

"What will they do if I don't?" she responded. She discovered, then and there, that such behaviour caused one to be sent to the Mother Superior.

Thus, from that moment on, she refused to wear her hat and it wasn't long before she was summarily brought before the Mother Superior. Beatrice finally had her chance to explain her circumstances.

And so her opportunity to return home came and for a moment there was a great joy in Frances Street, for no one knew where she had been.

Not long after this adventure, Beatrice married her childhood sweetheart Walter. For a time, they found lodgings at Pop and Nana Friday's house in Somerset Street. Then Iron Ford died and not long after that Agnes became poorly. Walter, like his father before him, went to sea. While he was away, Beatrice did not know what to do about her mother. She decided to take her to the

My mother Beatrice in her youth.

nuns with whom her mother had worked so much when she was young. Much to Beatrice's surprise, the nuns found themselves unable to help. So Agnes saw out her last days in St David's, which at that time was a Poor House referred to as the City Lodge.

In the meantime, with both of Beatrice's parents deceased, Twist had made every effort to secure 19 Frances Street for himself, preventing Beatrice from inheriting her rightful legacy. When Walter came home from sea, he and Beatrice went to the police to see what could be done but discovered there was no law preventing him from staying. But, in sympathy, the officer suggested to Beatrice that she could do what Twist had done and then the law would work the same for her.

So, they stood with suitcases in hand in Canal Parade, around the corner from Frances Street, waiting for Twist to leave. Once he had gone, they quickly ran inside and set up house and home and when Twist returned told him to go to the police.

19 Frances Street was to be their home until the early 1960s, when Tiger Bay was to undergo another sustained attack upon its community integrity with the organised demolition of its Victorian structures. This will be more fully elaborated upon in Chapter Seven, "Nuclear Bomb on Tiger Bay."

But before we close the chapter on Old Tiger Bay, there is still more to tell.

Chapter Three

TIGER BAY — THE MOVIE

In the previous chapters an attempt was made to capture the character and resilience of the people of Tiger Bay in the face of ostracism, negative publicity and general hardship. Of course, hardship has never been unique to Tiger Bay. The earlier part of this century was difficult for all communities throughout Britain that had to endure the vicissitudes of two Wold Wars. But the majority of the other communities, perhaps with the exception of Liverpool Eight and parts of London, were relatively homogeneous. Tiger Bay, on the other hand, had a mottled dab of every nationality, religion and race you can think of. Throughout the hard times, it managed to remain, with all its differences, a coherent and integrated community.

It is this characteristic of lengedary togetherness that unbaised visitors have discovered on many a sojourn to the area, adding a positive dimension to the legend of Tiger Bay. The media, over the course of the 20th century, have not always taken a negative view of Tiger Bay: sometimes, they have made favourable observations. Also, film makers have more than once come to Tiger Bay to shoot movies or documentaries there or to find extras for the exotic background of the movies they were making. Stories of those events are still retold by the older generations in Tiger Bay. What follows is an attempt to recapture those times.

In pre-television days, going uptown to the "pictures" was a thrilling event for Bay Boys and Girls alike. However, although there were no cinemas in Tiger Bay, we didn't always have to go uptown to see a film.

On Thursday nights the Wesleyan Church, a wonderful grey stone building with an inviting flight of stone steps leading up to its entrance, raised a screen before the altar. And there before our eyes, all for "thrupence," was our Thursday night picture. Nowadays, this church no longer stands in South Loudoun Place. In its place one finds a small, architecturally unimpressive chapel.

The Wesleyan Methodist Church in Old Loudoun Square, where the films of Paul Robeson were shown.

Mr Webster, pastor of the Loudoun Square Wesleyan Church, and his family lived in their home next to the church. Thanks to Pastor Webster, we Bay Boys and Girls became educated by some very relevant films. Of course, there were also a lot of films that were just pure entertainment. Two that stand out in my mind, because they played so regularly, are "Proud Valley" and "Sanders of the River." Both these films featured Paul Robeson, who had made them in Britain during the 1930s while in exile from the United States, owing to his stand against American racism. With his marvellous voice Robeson found a great "welcome in the hillside" and sang with many a Welsh male-voice choir. This aspect of his sojourn in Wales was represented in the film "Proud Valley." I always cried in that film — when fire broke out in the mine and all the men were trapped. But, of course, one had to hide ones tears lest the others think you a "big baby." After all, it was the fifties!

Billboard film poster from the 1930s.

Paul Robeson also found a welcome in Tiger Bay, where he made several visits to the Jason home on the west side of Loudoun Square. There he used to visit the African American, Aaron Mossell, who lodged with the Jason family at that time in 9 Loudoun Square. In actuality, Mr Mossell was uncle by marriage to Paul Robeson. No doubt that relationship was one of the reasons he came to visit. Nowadays, Mossell would be referred to as a Black activitist cum-communist, just as Paul Robeson, himself, had many times been so regarded. Even so, this American film actor thrilled us immensely, because he had a wonderful voice and had the essential quality of being black. He was someone like us — at least for those of us of African descent! It must be recalled that in the media of those days one rarely saw a black face that wasn't a white face painted black with white eyes and mouth. As late as the 1950s, Black artists did not even appear on the covers of record albums they recorded.

Walking home through the park in Loudoun Square, I stepped on a leaflet advertising the film "Carmen Jones," featuring Dorothy Dandridge and Harry Belafonte. The announcement said that the film was playing at the Park Hall Cinema. The mere sight of the leaflet sent shudders of excitement

Aaron Mossell, in easy chair, at his Loudoun Square lodgings in the Jason home, in conversation with his friend Edward Bovell. (Circa 1950.)

through me.

Not many years later, "Black Orpheus," the Brazilian version of the Greek myth, was showing at the Odeon Cinema in Queen Street. And, there was even a film about a clash of cultures called "Man of Two Worlds," where a Europeanised African returns home to his native land. However, for us, the main feature was the fact that the fire dancer, who appeared in the film, was the cousin of Olwen Blackman, Joey Pereira! "At last! We're in the pictures!" was the general feeling of the time.

In Tiger Bay, of course, Paul Robeson was well known. Not only had he been in Wales the decade before I was born, but many of the extras in the film "Sanders of the River," made in London's Elstree Studios, came from Tiger Bay. We all knew that the witchdoctor, dancing wildly in the centre of the film's version of an African village, was Mr Graham, the "Bengal Tiger," from Sophia Street. And, that was Uncle Willy Needham leaping around in the loincloth, which he kept for years after the film was made! (That loincoth was bright red, though one could not tell it in the black and white movie.) And we all waited silently for the river boat song to being so we could all join in. "Iyee ako, Iyi ge de," we would all chant in unison with Paul and all the African boatment. Only we would be going through the motions of rowing in our church seats!

Some 20 years after "Sanders of the River" was made, if

A youthful Paul Robeson, star of "Proud Valley" and "Sanders of the River."

you happened to be passing the timber float, which was a little south of West Canal Wharf, you might see a gang of "Bay Boys' on a separated timber log rowing across the lake singing the River Boat Song. You also might see the "Dockee" chasing them in his rowing boat, pointing his long wooden oar with the hook on the end, which was used to fish out any misfortunate youngster who fell into the timber float. Unfortunately, that hook had to be used on more than one occasion!

Then there was the scene where Paul sang the lullaby to the little black baby in his arms. That was Deara Williams' first film debut. Deara was born of an Afro-Celtic mother, whose mother was Irish. Deara's mother married Philpot Williams, an African, a Kru man of Liberia, known as "Mr Philpot," and from him she inherited her rich African features. Like Danny Sinclair of Peel Street, Mr Philpot kept a gambling house in Christina Street, where many an African, who wanted to try his luck, would find himself frequenting.

Deara, like my sister Leslie, was among the many Bay children who were evacuated to Aberdare and other places in the South Wales valleys during the Second World War, due to heavy bombing over the Docklands. Deara's back bedroom in Tiger Bay faced the rear of the houses on Bute Street. During the course of the war, gerry bombs eventually hit buildings in Bute Street and her whole back bedroom window was blown

Local singer of Indo-Cymric descent, Rohima Ali, in cabaret during the late 1950s.

into the bedroom. The enormous blast caused absolute terror in poor Deara. Events like these led to the evacuation of the youth of the community.

Shortly after the war, most of the evacuees returned home from the Valleys. However, Deara didn't return to Tiger Bay until she was 15. And, when she did, she was very black and very Welsh!

Deara's first days at South Church Street School weren't too joyful with her having such a strong Welsh accent and speaking Welsh too! But soon she obtained the Tiger Bay Cardiff accent and was once again initiated as a "Bay Girl." Her peers included Irenie Spettie, Margaret Freeman, Rohima Ali, Maureen Jemmett, Mahala Davis, Iris Freeman, Patti Flynn and Shirley Bassey, to name only a few. Like so many of this age group, these Bay Girls were destined for show business. At least they thought so.

In Deara's case, show business became a reality. She went on to be a dancer in London, studying with Boscoe Holder, brother to the famous Afro-American choreographer, Geoffrey Holder. She became an exotic dancer, with an act that included a boa constrictor. It was while doing this act, touring in Spain with a circus that she found her way on to the movie set of "The Last Days of Pompeii." This was the version with

Another cabaret artist from Old Tiger Bay, Patti Flynn (née Young). Now living on the Iberian Peninsular.

Steve Reeves and Christine Kaufman. Whenever this movie is shown, for a few moments, while Caesar eats his grapes, one can see Deara, clad in Roman attire, doing the Tiger Bay Stomp, a circular rhythmic movement, snake and all.

Another early film that featured a Tiger Bay lovely was the first "Cleopatra" with Claudette Colbert. Chrissy Sinclair, mentioned in Chapter One, known to her friends in London (where the film was made) as Marie, played an Egyptian musician with a lily on her head. By her presence in this film, Chrissy, a brown-skinned "Bay Girl," added a touch of authenticity to the film's portrayal of ancient Egyptian society.

And then there was J Lee Thompson's "Tiger Bay" — the film that starred Hayley Mills, John Mills, Yvonne Mitchell, Horst Buchholtz, the community of Tiger Bay as extras, and me! I was the boy that fought with Hayley in the film and prevented her from playing with us down at the Pier Head.

"Get back to London, Gilly Evans. You don't belong down here!" were some of my famous lines. Other members of the local community in this scene included Royston Casanova of the Dixon/Pearce clan, who gained international fame after a large family photograph of them — captioned "The Rainbow Family" — was published in the late 1980s. Also, there was Lesley Mansbridge from the Dudley Place area in the Docks.

I remember being quite peeved at the time with Father Brian Oman. J Lee Thompson wanted me to appear in the wedding scene inside the Church of St Mary the Virgin alongside Mr Pine and Norman "Oscar" Walker in the choir. As it was, I used to be a choir boy throughout my youth but Father Oman was upset that I had deserted the choir in my adolescence. He would not let me don the cassock anymore, not even for a film.

Two wet weeks were spent creating that five minutes on screen on the Pier Head ramp, where in its heyday passengers boarded the Campbell Steamers for Weston-Super-Mare or Ilfracombe. For most of the two weeks, John Mills chaperoned and helped to direct his, at that time, very young daughter.

Me and Haley Mills in J Lee Thompson's 1959 film, "Tiger Bay," made in 1958. Scene taken at the Pier Head.

Prior to auditioning for the role in the film "Tiger Bay," my friend Anthony Evora and I had been enrolled as students at the College of Music and Drama, which in those days — the late 1950s — was located inside Cardiff Castle. I am sure this background had a lot to do with my selection for the part. At that time, my ambition was to be in the theatre. As for Anthony, having seen "The Dam Busters," on one of the occasions when Dean-Dean took us to the pictures, being an airforce cadet was all he dreamed of. Eventually, Anthony joined the Royal Air Force — just prior to the demise of Old Tiger Bay.

"Tiger Bay" is the film most loved by the local inhabitants — not so much for its story, although the story is quite enthralling, but for its scenery and the memories it evokes.

"Get back to London, Gillie Evans!" I said. The Pier Head scene from "Tiger Bay" with Haley Mills and Michael Anderson, Jr in centre.

Now we've always known that Herbert Street is not actually in Tiger Bay, but we still thrill to see our Junie Fettah calypsoing down that street in the wedding celebration to the strains of "Never Make A Pretty Woman Your Wife." And, of course, everyone knows you can not go down the West Junction Canal and end up on the Newport Suspension Bridge twelve miles away. But then again that's cinematic license!

Reviewing this film is virtually the only way those of us who remember can see the actual streets we used to walk upon. Beloved Loudoun Square, dilapidated though it was from the damage done in World War II and the ravages of time, is permanently and absolutely captured in this black and white film.

Interest in Tiger Bay — the movie — was rekindled during the mid-eighties when "The Dream That Kicks" was being produced for Channel 4. This four-part programme reviewed the films made in and about Wales in the history of film making. The latter part of the series examined the making of "Tiger Bay."

Clare Pollack, a television producer from London working on the aforementioned programme, was excited as she left Cardiff General Station and asked the first person she could see: "Which way it is to Tiger Bay!" Only to discover the Tiger Bay she was in search of was a mere shadow of the one in the movie. Nevertheless, "The Dream That Kicks" was able to juxtapose the locations in the film with the locations as they are today. The programme also managed to capture some of the bitterness we feel at the loss of our original community integrity caused by the demolition of the old structures and dislocation of our families.

Entering Loudoun Square. Another scene from the movie "Tiger Bay." The dark figure at left is German actor Horst Buchholtz.

Thus, in more ways than one, we owe a debt of gratitude to J Lee Thompson for filming that story in the "Tiger Bay" setting. It has become something of a classic for the older generations among us to relish.

Apparently, Tiger Bay — place and the film — had a similar effect on Mr Thompson. He is in America at present involved in a remake of "Tiger Bay" in Hollywood. I can not help wondering who is going to play me! And, ultimately, one can only wonder how the new film's future success will compare with that of its namesake!

Chapter Four

UP THE BAY, DOWN THE DOCKS!

To those that know, Tiger Bay began at Old North Church Street and ended at Hodges Row. This tiny enclave of small streets, each with its own pub (with the exception of Old Christina Street), was readily distinguished from the community further south. The boundaries were well known in Old Tiger Bay days, as indicated by the fact that those who lived south of Mount Stuart Square — in Louisa Street, South Williams Street and Evelyn Street, to name a few — would always say they were going "up the Bay," when they visited friends there, while those in "The Bay" always said they were going "down the Docks." Now, back then, "Down the Docks" there was a Spanish community that predominantly lived in Old George Street. And it only seems appropriate to remember our "Spanish Days" in the once thriving international community that was Tiger Bay.

For those who don't recall, George Street was immediately behind the "Packet" pub in Bute Street and ran from James Street to Stuart Street. George Street had two pubs. Closest to James Street was the "Castle" and at the end beyond the Library was "Ye Old Pilot," once run by Marie (pronounced "Marry") Gomez. In the Pilot, Spaniards could have a dance (dancing was not permitted in all pubs) as Marie Gomez had a dance licence.

Also in George Street, you would have found Perez' Wine Shop, Josefina ("Josie") Hormaechea's famous salt fish shop (aromas are still recalled by local inhabitants) and a Spanish restaurant. You would have also heard names like Juana, Lupe, and Consuelo Dos Santos shouted in the street. (My childhood friend Merced Martin was descended from this

47

Bute Street showing Maria Street Police Station, where police actually lived with their families.

background.) The Spanish seamen "Down the Docks" were not only shopkeepers, many were in business as chandlers, as were many Italian seamen.

As for Josefina Hormaechea, she also served meals to seamen who fancied a meal in her big family kitchen. According to her grandson Lorenzo Del Gaudio, at any given time, twelve to fourteen people would be sat around the huge oak table in the room behind her saltfish shop. On one particular day, she served a seaman her usual fare. That seaman was Aristotle Onassis. Of course, he wasn't the rich shipping magnate he is today when he came to eat in Tiger Bay.

Our Nora Glasgow, being born there in 1925, has dear memories of George Street as a Spanish community. Hers was one of the first families to live in George Street, who were not of Spanish background. Her family was followed by Juliana of the Ali family, famous for their "Bombay" restaurant, which stood at the end of West Bute Street, near James Street, located almost opposite "Bab's Bistro," now Mrs Brown's "Caribbean Restaurant." These days, you can find the Bombay in Rhiwbina under a different family management. Another Indo-Cymric Ali family resided on this street, as its Spanish flavour began to diminish. Ronnie and Valerie Ali I remember with great affection as childhood friends.

If we leave the Docks and go "Up the Bay," we cannot forget Manuela, who for me epitomised Spain. On any fair weather day, Manuela's chair was placed outside her house in Old Angelina Street, at the corner of Sophia Street right opposite Kerrigan's Marchioness of Bute. On that corner, in those days, was found the largest congregation of people outside of Loudoun Square Park. There, Manuela sat, dressed in her floor-length black skirt with her shawl wrapped about her shoulders, observing the gamblers rolling the dice outside Kerrigans. Like so many other ladies seated outside their houses, Manuela observed the corner of Bute Street to see if Bobbies, making their rounds from Maria Street Police Station, where they actually resided with their families in those days, were coming. "Heads Up" was the signal shouted if the Bobbies appeared and in all the excitement money and dice disappeared before you could say "Paul Robeson."

Maria Deroche (left) and neighbour talking together in Old Sophia Street in the early 1950s. Between them Berlin's "Milk Bar" and the "Zauwia" next to it can be seen. Where the man leans on the lamppost is its intersection with Old Angelina Street.

When Manuela passed away, Valerie Romaine and I watched as her king size brass bed was being moved out.

"Oh! Look at the bed!" We laughed, having been conditioned to believe that furniture of that sort was so old fashioned. This was the time when everyone was getting rid of their brass fireplace ware in favour of the "modern" tiled fireplaces. After our modern fireplace was installed, the usefulness of those old Victorian fireplaces soon dawned upon my mother. The realisation came once she discovered she could no longer put the kettle on the fire, make toast or bake things in the side oven, which was no longer there! Furthermore, it wasn't long before the comtemporary furniture was falling apart and our good old well-made Victorian furniture, some of which was already close to 100 years old when I was born, was now viewed as antique. The brass fittings that we had been induced to regard as old fashioned were now high priced "objects d'art" in the shops in Mill Lane.

Excitement on Kerrigan's corner was never very far away, as Johnnie Lima and I were to witness once while swinging on a rope tied around the bar at the top of the street gas lamppost, taking this adventure in turns with Michael Harmon and Anthony Evora. Suddenly, out of a crowd of gamblers congregating under Kerrigan's window, Ozzie Taylor came running hell bent for leather. Literally running for his life! Dressed really sharp, like Bay Boys did, in his best shot silk suit. His shoes left behind at the open air casino. He, running bare foot to Loudoun Square. Somali, knife raised in hand, in hot pursuit. Me and Johnnie Lima stared in amazement as they fled by and alarm was sounded down Old Angelina Street.

Doors flung open as Aunty Sarah, Aunty Gladdie, Francis Evora, Eddie Bob, and Nellie Webb rushed out to see what all the commotion was about. Everyone rushed down to Loudoun Square. However, by that time Ozzie had made it home. (His house was second from the end on Loudoun Square at the corner of Old Angelina Street.) Door shut behind him, Ozzie was now safe. Nonetheless, the Somali still flung his knife at the strong wooden door of the Taylor home, succeeding in splitting the door — as Dorothy, Ozzie's sister, noticed after all the excitement had died down. All the street was filled with the general oohs and aahs.

"Did you see that!"

"Boy, that Ozzie could run!" And laughter mixed with every retelling.

In those days, poor Dorothy rarely ventured past her front door, her father, Mr Taylor, being so strict. Of all the Taylor brothers, Ozzie and Raymond were close friends to Ronnie, my brother, and Raymond was often in Frances Street spending the night at our house hiding from the wrath of his father. Recently, Ozzie passed away and in St Mary's Church during his funeral, if you looked carefully among the congregation, you would have noticed a Mohammedan, Mohammed Omar, paying his respects, the very same Somali who, so many years before, had pursued him.

Mrs Jeffrey's grocery shop where I bought my father's black-eye peas.

So, the gambling activity on the corner of Sophia Street and Old Angelina Street added a great deal of excitement. Sophia Street's intersection with Christina Street was equally interesting. On one corner was Mrs Jeffrey's Grocery Shop. I loved going in her shop to

Khaid Salah's shop on Old Christina Street with customers Lilly Taylor and daugher, Ronnie. Taken in 1950. Note the save Palestine fund box on the shelf.

get black-eye peas when my mother wanted to cook them with rice for my father. Opposite Mrs Jeffrey's was Gunderson's Fish & Chip Shop, where every kid in Tiger Bay, at one time or another, climbed underneath the counter to hide and play while Mrs Gunderson served her many customers who asked for "Sixpenneth of chips, please." There we would stay until Mr Gunderson thought it was time to chase us away. Then there was Mrs Earl's Sweet Shop on the opposite corner, outside of which one never failed to find housewives gossiping or congregating, some wrapped in long shawls creating a modicum of privacy while they breast fed their babies, rocking to and fro.

Finally, the Butcher Shop on the south corner was once run by Hameeda Said's mum, Aggie-The-Butcher. Later on, it was run by Ethel Adeni, a lovely and humble Welsh lady married to an Arab it was said from Aden. Mr. Adeni was very fond of children and adopted a few, which were raised in his home in Christina Street much closer to the Loudoun Square end of the street. Khaid Salah's grocery shop and another Arab shop were also in Christina Street between Sophia Street and Loudoun Square as well. When he wasn't attending the Zauwia on Sophia Street next to the Milk Bar or the little white minaretted Noor al Islam Mosque in Peel Street for prayers, Mr Adeni taught Arabic to the Muslim children of Tiger Bay in a make-shift school house in Gladstone Street, next to where Patsy Clark kept his coal stored when he wasn't delivering. (Gladstone Street was a cobblestoned street on the corner of which was the House of Blazes, a somewhat infamous pub. Unfortunately, upon those cobblestones we can no longer walk.)

On the corner of Peel Street, opposite the Arab School, was the home of "Kitty Said," a Cardiff girl, who had many years before married Mr Mohammed, an Egyptian. Now, Kitty's husband was called Said Mohammed but the Sinclairs were in the habit of calling Mr. Mohammed Mr Said (pronounced "Side") and that is how Kitty became known as Kitty Said. Mary, Farida, Said, Gaynor and Mona were their Tiger Bay-born Egyptian children. Living in Peel Street, they were naturally friends of the Sinclair and James families despite the

Enjoying a drink together in the mid-1950s, Gaynor and Mary Mohammed, sisters, alongside their Peel Street neighbour, Helen Sinclair, my aunty.

Old Bute Street as it was heading north to town. Near the lorry can be seen the entrance to the very lively Freemasons Pub at the corner of Loudoun Place. Just a little further up was Lilly Volpert's Haberdashery.

Muslim and Christian difference. Religious differences never interfered in Tiger Bay life anyway and so I spent a great deal of my life in their house. Many was the day we rolled up the carpet in their front room so we could dance to all the latest Rhythm & Blues records and it was in that room that we all learned to do the Cha Cha Cha to Perez Prado's "Cherry Pink & Apple Blossom White." Once in a while, I would be "look out" for Mr Mohammed if Mary or Gaynor were cooking up a bacon sandwich when desperate for a "Christian meal."

Also "Up the Bay," there was a part of Bute Street alongside Loudoun Square where once thrived such commercial activities and institutions as Dickie Diamond's Dairy, Corne's Seamen's Clothes, the Seamen's Mission, Moore's Jewellers, Colpstein's, Volpert's and Louis Fennig's Butcher Shop. There was also the Adelphi pub next door to which you would find the Canadian Cafe, commonly known as "Chic Chicalos," next to where you would find a side door leading to

Mr Graham, the "Bengal Tiger," and family of Sophia Street. Clara May, known to one and all as "Mingo," stands watching in the back.

No 182 Bute Street, the house where Shirley Bassey was born. Such a talent as hers, is the result of the West African heritage of Tiger Bay where Calabar, Kru, Igbo, Mende, Soso and Yoruba seamen met Celtic and Anglo-Saxon brides, whose living descendents, with African sounding names like the Mbakwes of Old Evelyn Street and the Sangos of Old Hodges Row, can still be found, along with some not so African sounding names, like Boston, Davids and Glasgow. Add to this the Caribbean connection and in the streets "Bengal Tiger,"

The steps upon which Tiger Bay children once danced and played. Originally a Welsh Presbyterian Chapel, the church became known locally as the Finnish Church.

"King of Beasts," "Coloured Eva," and "Black Dolly" are some of the nicknames you would have heard. And, if we go back far enough in time, you would have heard Welsh speaking families on the west side of Loudoun Square who used to attend the Old Welsh Church opposite the Wesleyan Methodist Church (where, as mentioned in the previous chapter, we used to see Paul Robeson in "Sanders of the River" and "Proud Valley" on Thursday nights for thrupence) where now stand the Butetown Health Centre and St Paul's Church, respectively.

Another interesting church, long gone from the Tiger Bay scene, was the Finnish Church, located in Hannah Street. Greco-Romano pillars graced this building with steps leading up to its entrance upon which many children danced, long after the church had fallen into dereliction. The Johansens, who had lived there, returned to Finland during World War II.

Bute Street had a great deal of character and a great many characters. Whiling away the time on one of its corners, you would notice some familiar local characters who frequently passed by. Kids often stopped playing in their streets to see "Norman," if the word was out he was about. Norman always walked with stately dignity down Bute Street towards the Docks, well-dressed with his brown trilby hat cocked to one

Tiger Bay's own, Joey Erskine, winning the cup.

side and never without make-up on his face and a newspaper rolled up under his arm like a ladies handbag! Clearly, we lived in tolerant times, because he came to no harm in Tiger Bay. Where he came from, where he went is not known, but he was a well-known familiar character on Bute

Teddy Best of Old Loudoun Square at the height of his boxing career in the 1950s.

Street.

Then there was Winnie Graham of Sophia Street. Cat-like eyebrows and an 18" waist. Extremely high stiletto heels and gorgeous chocolate brown legs on show beneath a scandalously short mini-skirt. But really there was no scandal. Winnie was just 10 years before her time. A decade later, no girl in Britain or the rest of the world was dressed unless she was in a mini-skirt. Winnie was Tiger Bay's avant guard!

Another well known talent came from the aforementioned Sango family. Redvers Sango was a light-heavyweight, who, like Joey Erskine, was a boxing champion and held the Welsh light-heavyweight title as well as the Aldershot District

The Loudoun ("Pub") Hotel on old Bute Street, where Johnnie Erskine was landlord during the early 1950s. Once located between Hodges Row and South Loudoun Place.

title, the Southern Command championship and the Army and Imperial Services Boxing Association light-heavyweight crowns. The Hodges Row, where he was born, was somethimes locally referred to as "Sango's Row." Further up Bute Street, next to San On Yen's Restaurant, lived Mrs Florie Fernandez's adopted son, Phil Edwards, who was also a well-known fighter of the time. And, while we are on the subject of fighters of the day, we must not overlook Loudoun Square's Teddy Best.

But, returning to Hodges Row, only a few houses were left on this street in my young days. The old Chinese laundry

on the south corner at Bute Street, opposite Johnnie Erskine's "Loudoun" pub, was long closed, sealed and painted green. Beyond these little homes was the "Barrel Field," an over grown area where every child in Tiger Bay found adventure. Inside and beyond the Barrel Field was a lock that held a small basin of water for the boats that used to travel the Glamorganshire

Leslie Sinclair seated on the canal lock at Hodges Row in Old Tiger Bay.

Canal. And how we children loved to play in that lock and by the Canal, even though those territories were strictly forbidden by our parents. As it happened, many a child lost its life to the Canal and to the timber float at the top end of Canal Parade.

Being restricted territory, no one could afford to let their parents know that they had been over there. So, if you got mud on your shoes or your clothes got wet, you had to clean your shoes and light a fire to dry your clothes before you could go home. Mind you, there was always somebody who would snitch on you or have to tell because they thought you were drowning. This happened to Billy Sinclair. As a youth, he fell into the Canal and someone rushed to his home to tell his mother, Mary Ann, that he had been drowned. Billy, however, had climbed out of the Canal and was busy drying his clothes by a fire so he could go home with no one the wiser.

In the meantime, Mary Ann got the news. Mrs Harris and another elderly matriarch were required to hold her up as she screamed up to God while being aided down Peel Street to make the journey to the Canal in search of her lost boy. As was typical in those days, many people from the Bay followed behind and went over the Canal to witness the tragedy.

As Billy had nearly dried his clothes and was about to go home, he saw the crowd of people and went to see what it was all about. There in the middle was his mother, barely able to stand, were it not for her two devoted supporters, until her eye caught hold of Billy standing there in all his glory, very much alive.

"You little bugger!" she screamed, her strength fully recovered as she chased Billy every inch of the way home to Peel Street, swearing to murder him once they got home for putting her through so much agony. But then that was a day in the life of Tiger Bay.

On the corner of Bute Street and Old Sophia Street, you would find Mr Wing's "Sam On Yen" restaurant. Mr Wing was "Sam On Yen" to us. (Whether it really was his name has only now occurred to me.) He was the owner of the first Chinese restaurant in Cardiff. In my day, Sam On Yen, a lovely old man, who sometimes wore a bowler had and striped trousers, was the last remnant of a once thriving Chinese community in Tiger Bay. Of course, his restaurant was the last Chinese restaurant in the Bay. Tales of Chinese laundries fronting Opium Dens are legendary but, nonetheless, in some instances true. Before my time, one used to be opposite the Loudoun Pub on Old Hodges

Row. Chinese games were played inside as well as opium ingestion but apparently no harm done.

"From the Golden Cross pub in Custom House Street all the way down Bute Street to the Windsor Esplanade you could find Maltese family homes, business establishments and cafes," said old Louis Lobina, whose memories of old Tiger Bay go way back to his youth. And he is correct. I, too, remember Camileri's Shop, "Chippies" and the Maltese Boarding House on Bute Street opposite "Sessions Bridge" facing Sophia Street. Discarded peanut shells, scattered on the pavement in front of the Chemist Shop just below the boarding house, indicated that a group of Maltese men had just recently been whiling away the time there. I still recall Junie Fettah, a Tiger Bay Girl descended from an Egyptian, besotted with love for her Maltese seaman fiance, as she knocked the door of the boarding house in search of her husband to be.

On the bridge leading down to town, just south of the Bridge Hotel, the pub where Horst Buchholtz hid the gun in the movie "Tiger Bay," you could find the home of the Farruggias, a Welsh-Maltese family related to Peggy who, however, was raised on Sophia Street. Nowadays, Peggy makes numerous literary contributions to the local newspapers and remains a staunch advocate of old Tiger Bay community unity.

Further down stood the old "George Cross' Community Centre, named in honour of Malta's contribution to the war effort in its defence of British interests during World War II. This long single-storey bungalow housed many a community function that had nothing to do with Malta, like dances and the meetings of the "Sons of Africa." It stood next to a field that was all that remained of several buildings that had suffered a direct hit by Hitler's bombs. This bombed-out site had once been the home of the Delgado family and also the Scandinavian Seamen's Home. And the tragedy of the loss of the beautiful Miriam, daughter of Maria Deroche, who was killed along with her father during the direct strike, her body being thrown completely across Bute Street onto the railway lines of the Taff Vale Railway, is still recalled by older members of the community.

In my youth, one could still see the remains of the air raid shelters in the rear of the field, which made an ideal place for children's games long before there were such things as adventure parks.

In those days, talk of Prime Minister Dom Mintoff could be heard. But then came Malta's independence and Tiger Bay was robbed of many who returned to their homeland, taking away a great deal of Mediterranean character that is still sorely missed.

Since the late 1950s, the Arabs, Somalis and Africans in general have been quite different in character from those that contributed to the foundation of Tiger Bay as a community. Those seamen of the early days were, in fact, mostly peasants coming from upriver villages that were tribal oriented. Many still had tribal scars upon their faces and they spoke English as they saw fit to speak it.

"Which side you da sleep las' night!" meaning "Where did you sleep last night," you might hear one say to the other when he saw that his friend left early in the morning from a house in which his wife did not live.

"Walikum salaam," said one Arab to another, in response to "Salaam Alikum," passing each other in the street.

"Wurria," a Somali would say when referring to the other as "brother."

A consequence of all this multi-lingual chit-chat was that the kids in the Bay knew all these expressions regardless of their own ethnic background. "Hiya, Wurria," we would say, passing a Somali or "Salaam," to a passing Arab.

With the drawing to a close of the Colonial days in the late 1950s, Tiger Bay began to be visited by the "new" African, who came to Britain for an education. These were Africans with a part of the left side of their hair in emulation of the Englishman's hairdressing tradition of those days. They also spoke "perfect English," much to the enjoyment of Tiger Bay's youth, who always managed to respond to them in the lingo of the older Africans like Mr Wesley and Benno Johnson.

Growing up in Tiger Bay, we were used to all kinds of accents overlaid upon English, including the ever-present Cardiff accent. In this varied linguistic milieu, it was more than amusing to listen to visitors who knew very little English but could "talk Cardiff" when they needed to make themselves understood.

Of course, "Up the Bay and Down the Docks" had many other nationalities that we have not discussed. Portuguese, Greek, Turkish, Ukranian, Estonia, Scandinavian and other groups, although unmentioned here, nevertheless, made their cultural contributions to the many coloured tapestry of the very cosmospolitan community that was Tiger Bay.

Chapter Five

RHYTHM & BLUES IN TIGER BAY

The other night I happened to see the Sealy sleeping mattress television commercial — two people in bed sleeping to the lilting strains of "In The Still of the Night," a near perfect copy

of the song orginally sung by the American Rhythm & Blues group "The Five Satins." They made the tune a hit in the late fifties. Suddenly, it dawned on me that that song was never released in Britain at the time it was a hit. I knew about it, because the Black GIs stationed on American Bases in England such as Brize Norton, Fairford and Birddrup Park used to be in Tiger Bay practically every weekend and they brought their records with them for us to hear. We were privy to the very latest in Rhythm & Blues of the day. Sometimes, I would run up to Spillers Record Shop and ask Mr & Mrs Spiller for something by Shirley & Lee or some other group and discover that their records were still not released in Britain. If they could order the records and you finally got your copy of "Let The Good Times Roll," Mr & Mrs Spiller wondered in amazement where we had heard this music before. They soon became fans of Rhythm & Blues. I wonder where they are now?

Pamela Erskine on window sill, accompanied by weekend visiting GI, Andy Secreat, outside her home in old Angelina Street in July 1960.

The sound of the Kopy Kat "Five Satins" spun my mind back to those "good old days" and I remembered walking through Olwen Blackman's open front door in Old Loudoun Square. In those days, as has already been said, the front doors of the houses were always open. However, before seeing Olwen, I heard Priscilla Ankara's commanding voice ordering me to the front living room to listen as she put the needle on to a 45 and for the first time ever I heard Nina Simone sing "I Loves You Porgy." I stood and she sat — while knitting something in a big easy chair — and we listened transfixed as if hearing a prayer. In that same front room in Loudoun Square, I heard the Chantels sing "Every Night" and "The Plea," at a time when only "Maybe" had been released by that group in Britain.

A few years earlier, the Gospel and Blues singer Sister Rosetta Tharpe made an obligatory visit to Loudoun Square. She was on tour in Britain at the time and having been aware of the Tiger Bay legend had to see us for herself. I remember she threw a handful of coins into the air and we kids darted about trying to collect them.

A south side view of Loudoun Square with Olwen's mam, Lydia Blackman, and visiting GI, Billy Callender, seated on the park wall in the 1950s.

Tony Williams — lead vocalist of the Platters — at a party in the home of Rohima Ali in George Street in 1957. Immediately in front of him is Betty Neil and Margaret Freeman, to the far left. Singer Arthur "Gene Latter," Ford of Patrick Street is also present, at far right.

I always recall, one day when Zara Farrah was rushing down Canal Parade toward the Park. As she passed Frances Street and saw me with friends she said:

"You've got to see the picture uptown! Oh there's black people in it!"

We did. That picture was "Rock Around The Clock" and those black people were "The Platters." The Platters, like a number of other celebrities of the day, made many trips to Tiger Bay. After their many performances at the Empire Theatre in Queen Street, which is nowadays the C&A Department Store, they would come down to the Bay, where they had many friends. The Platters often ate at the "Bombay Restaurant" in West Bute Street where, at that time, the best curry in town could be found. Zola Taylor, the female singer in the group, was fast friends with Rohima Ali, whose family owned the

Bombay. Rohima, too, was a good singer and loved to sing "Misty," the song Dakota Staton had made very popular in the Bay (with her "Late, Late Show" album) before Johnnie Mathis or anyone else ever recorded it.

Momentarily, I recalled walking into Benno Johnson's Ghana Club that used to be on Bute Street, near the Adelphi Pub and Johnnie Erskine's Loudoun Pub. Inside, squeezed into that tiny venue, I saw half the Bay. Francis Davids, Jeannie Edwards, Olwen and many others were all swaying back and forth doing the "Cha Cha" to Jackie Wilson's "Lonely Teardrops." I couldn't wait to find a partner to join in admist the whooping and hollering that went with every dip or swoop down to the floor. Then I remembered seeing Margaret Freeman and her sister Daphne with a bunch of other Bay Girls, marching arm-in-arm down Bute Street, singing "Sincerely" at the top of the voices. If only the Moonglows could have heard them.

The Annexe on Bute Street with corner of Patrick Street in the distance. The little building in the center was better known as "Frenchies," where local talent learned to tap dance and where everyone went to dance on Friday and Saturday nights. The George Pub is next door behind the car.

On Friday or Saturday night in Frenchie's Annexe, you could hear Johnnie Ace sing "Pledging My Love" or Fats Domino sing "Blue Monday." You could also hear Calypso,

Mr French giving dance instruction to Lillie Sanders, Mary Beezar and Barbara Best closest to him.

Mambo and Merengue and do a West African High Life too! And Mr French, a long-term resident of Tiger Bay, who came from West Africa, taught local talent to tap dance. Everybody, as he said in his own inimitable way, could become a "Flim Star." And some did become stars, albeit not in films. Remember Irene Spetti, who used to sing as Lorne Lesley, and Patti Flynn? And, of course, there was "Bassey."

Shirley comes home. At the Rainbow Club in the late 1950s, Shirley Bassey, arm raised, enjoys the company of the youth of Old Tiger Bay.

67

When the Annexe closed at midnight and there was no where else to go, you could always find a welcome at Mrs Graham's on the corner of Sophia Street and Canal Parade. In that tiny little front room, Tiger Bay stomped the night away. There you could hear Ritchie Valens sing "La Bamba" or Sam Cooke sing "You Send Me" and you could listen to all the Rhythm & Blues groups you never heard on the BBC. And, if the electric went and there was not a "shilling" between us there was always Mrs Graham's pots and pans and Mingo could play mean quatro (four string guitar).

Another venue that closed at midnight, expelling its Bacchanalian night revellers into the streets of Tiger Bay in search of more fun, was the Cardiff International Athletic Club — known to everyone as the "CIACS" (pronounced "Kay-aks"). All opposing rugby teams, including the Fijians and Moaries, were entertained there after the game — no matter who won or lost. At that time, the club was located at the top of Bute Street, near Custom House Street, right next to the Bute Street railway bridge.

A staircase of several flights led you to the top floor where you would discover a dance floor that appeared to be bouncing away as the stomping Kayak reveller were enjoying a Saturday night revel. The Taylor Brothers, who could do a good Mills Brothers interpretation of "Up A Lazy River," were a regular feature — to the joy of all the members, who couldn't resist singing along. And, of course, the team had to sing the by then traditional round of "The River Boat Song."

Once out in the street, "the Boys" made there way to Old Loudoun Square and many a night in my back bedroom I wished I was old enough to go out and join them. You could hear them strumming guitars, singing risque calypsos like Lord Kitchener's "Kitch, Come Go To Bed" or doing their imitation of the Platters, to singing songs like Paul Anka's "Diana." The Diamonds' "Little Darling" and Roy Hamilton's "Unchained

Melody." In those days, there was definitely high life in Loudoun Square. But, sooner or later, the night would go quiet again.

The hottest teenage night spot in Tiger Bay, the "Sixpenny Hop," was located, would you believe, in the Old Vestry. (This building, which is still standing, once stood at the corners of North Church Street and West Church Street.) Scores of local youth queued up outside for the doors to open to hear Bobby Freeman sing "Do You Wanna Dance" or Danny and the Junior's "At The Hop." Thanks to Fathers Bradley and Lewis (both of St Mary's Church) and to Rita Ali (now in Denver, Colorado) and Sandra Cockle (now in Truro, Cornwall) and me, Tiger Bay kids had the best value for a "Tanner."

I remember when Joe Erskine ("Joey") won his fight. Crowds were around his door in Old Angelina Street, opposite the Bute Pub in Nelson Street. There, among the crowd was Clara Graham ("Mingo" to us) with guitar in hand, Hannah Graham and Pepsi (Peter Findlayson, that is). The crowd were all singing the calypso "Hold Him Joe!"

Johnnie Erskine with trilby cocked to the side in his own inimitable fashion and son, Joey, standing beneath lamppost. Sophia and Angelina Streets circa 1950.

Local resident Benny Bernard having coffee at Berlin's Milk Bar in Sophia Street in 1950.

When the excitement died down, you could always go to Margie Beezar's and Berlin's "Milk Bar" in Sophia Street — next door to the Zauwia, where local Arab youth learnt about Arabic culture and language — and play the records on the juke box. Bill Doggetts' instrumental "Honky Tonk" and Earl Bostic's "Flamingo."

As previously mentioned, subsequent to World War II and up to the demise of Old Tiger Bay, African American GIs (referred to as "Negroes" then) were constant visitors to Tiger Bay from the many American airbases throughout Britain.

But life being what it was in the 1950s, American-type racism had been transplanted from the United States to those bases, which ultimately created many problems. At base dances English girls had no objection to dancing with "Negro" Americans — which angered white American servicemen. This situation led to outbreaks of fighting between black and white servicemen on American bases in Britain. The Base Commander's solution was to initiate excursions of busloads of

More GIs visit Tiger Bay's Old Loudoun Square in the good old 1950s. Both, named Perry, clowning around with a six shilling bottle of VP wine. Note the bus, in front of the Welsh Church at the far right, that took Bay Girls to American Base dances.

"ladies of colour" to the weekend dances — so that Black American servicemen would have dance partners of their own kind.

One of these buses was a regular feature in Loudoun Square. It took Tiger Bay Girls to Brize Norton, Upper Heyford and other American bases throughout England. However, Tiger Bay Girls didn't mind dancing with white servicemen either. So, its seems the Tiger Bay tradition of racial harmony went a long way towards resolving the racial crises on American bases during the 1950s.

Even though these Black American GIs were the source of pride in Rhythm & Blues music, it must be remembered that in those days the word "black" was a fighting term. You didn't dare call someone "black" without expecting a fight of some sort.

In America the revolution to Black Consciousness had not even begun then, although decolonisation in Africa (and else where in the "Third World") was in full swing which is why Benno Johnson opened the Ghana Club in Bute Street in honour of Kwame Nkrumah, a leading and popular figure in the struggle against colonisation during the 1950s. Furthermore, West Indians and "Negro" Americans were preconditioned to believe that Africans were "savages," a message constantly inculcated into society by such movie genre as "Tarzan" and the like and the colonial propaganda of the time. So, when a Tiger Bay person acknowledged her origin in Africa and told a "Negro" American GI he was African too, she would find he was vehemently opposed to the idea.

We can say proudly in Tiger Bay that, thanks to the opportunity of being raised by or living amongst the humble African seamen, who made their homes here, we were well aware of our heritage long before Alex Haley's "Roots" informed the world about where we came from.

With the music dying down, I realised that what had just flooded my mind was only the icing on the Tiger Bay cake. Where has it gone? Why has it gone? There are so many reasons why, and after all things do change. But when we look back and realise what we've lost, I guess all we can say is what Fats Domino so aptly said way back then: "Ain't That A Shame?"

Chapter Six

MURDER IN OLD TIGER BAY

Nowadays, many who hear about life in the heyday of Tiger Bay believe they are being told of a fantasy spun and then viewed through the proverbial "rose-coloured glasses." For example, the previous chapter, "Rhythym & Blues In Tiger Bay," emphasised the music and fun side of life in Tiger Bay, perhaps leading one to believe this community had no troubles.

This opinion was expressed by a young African television documentary producer to Mrs Beatrice Sinclair, a veteran of all the vicissitudes visited upon Tiger Bay throughout the entire century. "Utopia!" he remonstrated, severely offending Mrs Sinclair, who was attempting to provide a true account of the past. However, Mrs Sinclair was not inventing a "Golden Age" myth. Tiger Bay was the multi-ethnic and international melting pot legend declared it to be. Such circumstances being so, it is quite probable that this narrative, too, will be falsely accused of spinning a yarn too incredible to be believed. Nonetheless, we shall venture on, wandering upon the same streets we encountered before, but this time we shall see what life was like in Tiger Bay in times of ill-fortune — when mischievous death stalked our otherwise secure "urban village."

Aunty Annie (Hannah) Gordon of Stuart Street in the Docks was the person who told me of the first murder in Tiger Bay that I recall. I have ever since visualised Mr Skyers wheeling the pram with his poor unfortunate victim, whom in a fit of rage he had beaten to death, rolled up in a carpet and wheeled over the wall into the sea. Unfortunately for him, the sea did not sweep her body out with the tide. Anyway, in Dudley Place in the early hours of that morning, a mother nursing her child suffering from measles just happened to be looking out of her window and saw Skyers pushing his pram.

On dark nights long after, many people still said they could hear the creaking wheels of Mr Skyer's pram as they quickly ran home to safety. In those days, many other phantoms also roamed the streets of Tiger Bay. What about the poor man coming home from town along Canal Parade one night? He was approached by a young lady in a long raincoat, who asked him for a light. Even in the dimly gas lit street, he knew something was amiss. When he lit the match, he saw something strange in her eyes. And, when he looked down, it was not feet he saw but hooves. Hooves! Hooves were all he could remember as he ran away.... It seemed every other street had a house that was haunted then.

During the 1950s, many in the community believe a dreadful miscarriage of justice took place and a local member of the Somali community was hanged for a crime, many local people believe, he did not commit. If memory served me right, I believe his was the last execution that took place in Cardiff up to this day. This incident involved the murder of Lilly Volpert, a Jewess, whose family was well known in the Bay and who ran a local Gentlemen's Outfitters & Haberdashery, near Zuzzen's Pawn Shop in Bute Street, which was also close to Colpsteins and the Freemasons public house at the corner of Loudoun Place. The murder itself was a scandal, as this was an exceedingly rare thing to occur in the community at the time.

I was a child when this incident occurred but later in my life, long after the event, I was to have an interesting or rather disturbing encounter that related to this case. I was in Streatham, London during the late 60s at the home of some friends, one of whom included a medium named Danny Sinclair. Besides the fact that this woman had the same name as my grandfather, yet was totally unrelated to me, she was very gifted in conducting seances. Initially, our being together had nothing to do with such matters but the subject became the topic of the evening and a group of us decided to prove whether these phenomena had any validity at all. Several attempts at contact took place. The details are not essential to our story, except to say that at some point during the five hours we communicated, Lilly Volpert was the principal party that spoke. Now, Ms Danny Sinclair had never set foot in Cardiff. But, to my astonishment, under the influence of Lilly Volpert's spirit, she spoke of the day Lilly was killed and named specific locations in Cardiff about which she could not have known. As if to completely deter credibility, Lilly kept referring to a moment after her throat had been cut. She communicated that as she lay strewn upon the shop floor "Satan" stepped over her body, went behind the counter and took money from the till. Often the spirits that communicate through mediums seem to use a tremendous amount of profanity, but in this case Lilly's spirit only did this when I asked or mentioned anything to do with the Somali, who was executed for her murder. She was clearly disturbed by this, as she vehemently insisted that this innocent man did no harm to her.

The following weekend I returned home to Tiger Bay and told all about this seance to my parents at our Saturday evening meal. My mother warned me about engaging in such activities, and as she didn't seem at all reasonable or rational about it, I proposed to say no more of it again.

However, at Sunday dinner my father, who was a church warden and officiated at St Mary's Church, had very surprising news to tell. Father Hall had asked my father to officiate at a funeral the following week. My father was concerned to know who had died and was told a Mr Gabe or man with some such name. Well, Dad didn't know anyone by that name but Father Hall insisted that he did. He said, "Don't you recall, Walter, all the children called him 'Satan.'" He was a dark-skinned West Indian who, it appeared, suffered from drinking too much. He always stood in front of the Freemasons and chased away the kids, who taunted him, with a walking stick. As it happened, on the exact night of the seance in London, "Satan" had taken severely ill and Zena Khan had to rush him to hospital in an ambulance that same night. He subsequently died.

Before he was hung for Lilly Volpert's murder, Mr Matan placed his hand upon the head of his youngest son and swore to Allah his innocence. The family of this executed man have been living in shame and dishonour in the Somali community both here and in Somaliland as a result of having such a grievous crime associated with them. (The family bears collective responsibility, as is Somali custom.) The family of Mr Matan still await exoneration from this shame.

The Noor Al Islam Mosque on Old Peel Street, where Tiger Bay's Muslims went to pray.

In those early day, when television had barely entered the community, an incident such as what happened to Lilly would be the topic of excited discussion for many years to come. But before the excitement was to lessen out of respect for Lilly, another tragedy soon occurred. This was the gunning down of Yusef Shurra, known to everyone in the Bay as "Mr Shay."

It seemed Mr Shay was a sort of banker and trusted confidant of many of the Mohammedan seamen in Tiger Bay. After all, many seamen could not read nor write — at least not in English. Besides looking after the affairs and interests of his fellow brothers in Islam, it was said he minded the money of seamen while they were at sea. This seems to be the fact that brought about his tragic end.

A young Somali seaman had come home to discover Mr Shay had recklessly spent money belonging to him and was unable to reimburse the lad. One can only imagine the young seaman's distress. It has been recalled by some members of the community that Mr Shay was supposed to send his money to the young man's family, who were suffering due to drought and had to pay for water. The young man, having received news that his family had not received the promised money, berated Mr Shay accordingly.

On Sophia Street corner this distraught young many questioned Mr Shay about the money while he was nonchalantly studying the horses in his newspaper. Mr Shay waved the young man away like a man being disturbed by a nuisance. Naturally, the man became distressed, and so he pulled out a gun, held it to Mr Shay's ear and pulled the trigger. As Mr Shay lay on the pavement, his assailant, in utter frustration, unbutttoned his trousers and urinated upon the fallen body.

Now, as mentioned in Chapter 4, it was the custom of the local men to gamble outside the Marchioness of Bute on the corner of Sophia Street and Old Angelina Street. In those days, Old Angelina Street was the hub of activity. It led one down from Old Maria Street to the Park in Loudoun Square. En route you passed the home of Billy Boston, the great Welsh rugby player (Mr Boston, Billy's father, was a "Soso" from Sierra Leone, West Africa; and his mother was Cardiff born.) You also passed by Billy Douglas' Fish & Chip Shop and, directly opposite Nelson Street, the home and birthplace of Joey Erskine. Next door was Polly Lopes' Sweet Shop. Poor Mrs Lope got "Polly" appended to her name because she kept a pretty parrot just behind the counter, which all the kids loved

Old Maria Street during the 1950s with Rose ("Roza") Duarte and her young cousin, Corinne Boston.

to talk to. Mrs Lope, a black "Portuguee" lady, was old ever since I can remember and wouldn't think twice about selling you a penny glass of pop. Immediately next door to her was Mary Ahmed's Shop, where penny drinks were also sold. This

Billy Boston — Welsh Rugby Champion in military uniform.

little sweet shop had a strange incense smell. A strange somewhat sinister appearing woman was Mary, her hair tied back in a bun in the Victorian fashion. I always wondered where the Arab bit came in, as Mary was quite a white lady. I guess she was married to an Arab some time in the distant past. Anyway, If you hurried on to the corner you would come to the "Bookies," where everyone bet their horses — of course, illegally then! What excitement when the Black Maria came to ar-

*John &
Nellie
Boston,
parents
of Welsh
rugby
player
Billy
Boston.*

rest everyone inside. The Bay Folk from all the streets would be out to watch!

This kind of excitement was the reason Leslie Sinclair, coming home for lunch from her Civil Service job on the Taff Embankment in Grangetown, decided against travelling down Canal Parade, the quickest way home, in preference for Old Angelina Street, which after all was the "Show of Life." As she walked alongside the hubbub created by the men rolling dice on the pavement, she suddenly heard a sound like a bottle of lemonade being opened. It wasn't until she saw the young Somali man waving a gun about in the air that she realised anything dangerous had occurred. Instantly, she ran home to tell her mother. Outside, on the pavement in front of the window of the Marchioness of Bute, lay Mr Shay having been shot directly in the head. Perhaps the young Somali had become so distressed from the circumstance of not having received the money due to him that the sight of Mr Shay in the street enraged him so much that he decided to pull the trigger and kill him. Who knows?

Soon after Mr Shay was shot, the streets were filled with people. Those who didn't know what had happened wanted to see. Among them was Mrs Beatrice Sinclair, who had just been informed by her daughter Leslie. Those who knew what had happened were trying to get away! Hearing the commotion, Johnnie Lima, Terry Walli and I ran out from Frances Street to approach Sophia Street only to witness Frances Evora, my friend Anthony's mother, with pinafore raised to assist flight, heading a crowd of fleeing people, screaming, "He's got a gun!" Soon the police were there but admist all the commotion it was the Bay Boys who subdued the irate assailant. Among them was Roy Corria, who clearly knew he faced no danger. It was at this point that Beatrice Sinclair arrived. She saw the assailant, a wretched and lamentable man, his eyes glaring into space. She witnessed him pacing up and down in his distress at the incomprehension of what he had just done. And as he was subdued, Beatrice felt compassion and hoped that no one would hurt him despite the fact that he had just killed a man.

Being as young as I was when this event occurred, I never knew what happened to the Somali seaman — whether he was convicted of murder or not. But in Tiger Bay this story can still be heard to this day.

Not every attempt at murder resulted in tragedy. Toward the end of the 1950s, there occurred another brush with death in Tiger Bay. This is the story of Michael Burrowes, sometimes known as the "Barracuda," who suvived to tell of it. (He more recently died an accidental death in London.) Mike left Cardiff many years ago leaving behind two sons, Alan and Junior [as well as other children from his previous marriage to Barbara Best], but they were not even born when this event happened.

It was the usual Friday night in Tiger Bay and I was passing through Loudoun Square on my way to Frenchie's Annexe for a dance. (The Annexe was just a short way down the Docks — in Bute Street, a little beyond Patrick Street.) The night, though dark, was lovely and the old trees in the Park arched over the street on the east side of the square lending a sense of cosy protection. The street lamp at the corner near the

Olwen Blackman (left) and Violet Bullen stand in front of a tree in Old Loudoun Square Park. To their right, in the background, is the Welsh Church as it was in 1951.

derelict old Welsh Church illuminated only the area immediately around it.

At that time, Mike was married to Barbara Wilson and lived with her at number 46 in the middle on the very same side of the square as the Welsh Church. They lived in the back room while Arthur Parris and family lived upstairs and Esmay Sumner and her son Owen lived in the front room facing the square. Mike and Esmay were both from Guyana and Mike treated Esmay like a sister and was also godfather to Owen. My uncle Tommy and his family lived a few doors down at number 40 at that time (before taking a branch of the Sinclair family to live in Llandaff North toward the end of the 1950s).

With the old families, one had a sense of belonging to them even when there was no blood relationship. The Wilsons were one of the oldest families in Tiger Bay and Barbara was like a relative to me.

Now, that night, as I climbed over the little grey stone wall that surrounded the park, I heard a commotion and loud shouting. Something in Somali. Something in West Indian English! What was going on? From the shadows to the light at the end on the corner people were coming. Then I saw Mike running past me, chasing after someone. As they approached the corner and entered the light, I saw the Somali turn back and fire a gun, but still Mike kept on running. I rushed to see what was happening as they turned toward the Wesleyan Methodist Church and, just as Mike reached out to grab the Somali, he fell. His body could not sustain the wound his mind was unaware that his body had sustained.

Doors and windows opened then. Esmay appeared at the front window. In fact, Joan Brown on South Loudoun Place was looking out of her window when the event occurred. Seeing the event taking place from her window, which was already open because her sister suffered from asthma and needed fresh air, she shouted to her sister to come and see. However, in complete disbelief at what Joan was saying, Valerie refused to move from her bed.

Meanwhile, crying, shouting and commotion prevailed. Barbara was in distress and, of course, eventually an ambulance was summoned. Among the crowd of community onlookers was an American GI, a friend of mine. He was very tall and always wore a military-type cap and dark sunglasses day or night, which is why he was called "Bebop." He was one of the many Black American GIs who made regular weekend visits to Tiger Bay during that time. I don't recall if there were others, but I remember that Bebop and I went up the stone steps that led into her house and spent the entire night consoling Barbara. However, "Babs" was emotionally strong, so it was quite possible she was consoling me. All of us were shaken from the attempted murder of one who was known so well.

I remember leaving that house and entering Loudoun

Square after the sun had risen, suddenly realising that my parents would be absolutely frantic that I hadn't come home the night before. However, when I got home and related the previous nights events to my parents nothing was said about my absence!

As can be seen, life was not always a bunch of roses in Tiger Bay but the community always rallied around in times of strife to help to make life easier to bear.

Alas, a time of great tragedy was rapidly approaching. One which, though difficult to see in advance, would involve the entire community for all time.

Chapter Seven

NUCLEAR BOMB ON TIGER BAY

Sometime in the 1950s, there was a nuclear explosion over Tiger Bay, though no one heard a sound. The detonation of this catastrophe was to bring utter devastation to those who survived to remember it. When it struck, the nucleus of old tightly knit families scattered like fragments to various outlying areas of Cardiff City in its fallout. A nuclear winter subsequently set in....

Such a dramatic metaphor for what happened to Tiger Bay during that time is the only way that seems to capture the magnitude of the pain inflicted on a community that was otherwise content to exist, as it had done up to that time, without interference from the outside world.

Nevertheless, the outside world had decided to interfere. According to an old man I met in Bristol, who had been an architect working on the project at the time, Cardiff City architects were planning the redevelopment — or, from our current perspective, the destruction — of Tiger Bay as early as 1954.

In bewilderment, many of us wondered what could have been the motivation? The condition of the structures in Tiger Bay, at that time, were no worse than those in Splott or Canton in the same period. Yes, Tiger Bay was blighted somewhat by war damage, but bombs dropped on Canton too! Yet, Canton remains but the structures in Tiger Bay do not.

It was as a child, on expeditions outside the Bay, that I heard remarks that Tiger Bay was thought of as a slum. Yet the home my family lived in was no slum, nor were many of the other homes I so often frequented. As a matter of fact, even though the movie "Tiger Bay" (during the scenes when Horst Buchholtz is in Loudoun Square) shows major disrepair and dilapidation on the north side of the square, Loudoun Square had spectacular buildings merely requiring refurbishing — Victorian and Edwardian buildings with high ceilings containing moulded features where chandeliers once illuminated the rooms. Given such a complete eradication of quite salvageable structures, one tends to be faced with the conclusion that the motivation was to dispose of the melting pot community that Tiger Bay represented. Over the years, many of us have come increasingly to see the "slum clearance" as — to borrow a phrase from Olwen Blackman — "municipal vandalism."

Was everything cherished, and all we had endured until now, to be eradicated? Had we fought and survived the First War of Tiger Bay (in 1919) in vain? Were the many hardships

Loudoun House & Nelson House, towerblock flats, rooted in the soil of Loudoun Square Park, where trees used to be. Note Kerrigan's Marchioness of Bute on the left. In earlier times, men would have gambled under the windows of the pub and, on the far right of the picture, Manuela would have sat outside her front door. Further down to Loudoun Square, on the right, the Westgate Pub can be seen on the corner of Frances Street, where I was born.

overcome to be forgotten? Was all that had happened to us as a community to disappear like the old beautiful trees of Loudoun Square, that knew our very innermost secrets, were to be uprooted?

When Nino Abdi stood watching as those trees were being pulled from the ground, he felt he knew it was the end. Those old trees were the very root of our community garden and the old greystone wall surrounding it the seat of many of our dreams. Were our dreams and our closely connected community to crumble with the wrecking ball?

During the post World War I period, despite the indifference of the city at large and the negative reports frequently published in the papers of the day, the Tiger Bay community had somehow survived — more unified than ever since the First War of Tiger Bay succeeded against the race rioters.

However, the City was not content that we were happy — in spite of the adversity imposed upon us by racially discriminatory policies that forced unemployment on most coloured merchant seamen. Local seafarers of every race made sure our tables were full. As it was, when we ventured out of Tiger Bay, we did not always receive the welcome that outsiders, who dared to come in peace, found when they came to us.

From our point of view, long before weapons of nuclear destruction existed, the City of Cardiff seemed hell bent on the destruction of Tiger Bay. Some in our community have expressed the opinion that the redevelopment was a device to rid the up and coming capital city of the 'blot' on the landscape. The City media generally encouraged this conclusion by regularly reporting damaging descriptions of life in our community. Even today such reporting is not infrequent. However, despite the municipal ostracism, Tiger Bay has endured: our community has evolved a sturdy tradition of survival, self-sufficiency and self discipline, against all the odds.

A child in Tiger Bay could not get up to mischief on any

of its streets without being chastised or even clipped "over the ear hole" by a totally unrelated adult, who would also give the child a really good telling off. Furthermore, no child dared to go home and say, "Mr or Mrs So-and-So" hit him or her. The response was always, "What did they hit you for? There must be a reason!" And, if you did not come up with an answer quick enough that bamboo cane, hanging on grandfather's picture on the living room wall, would soon come down on your backside. Unlike today, there was no "talking back" to adults then. You might have been made to black-lead the fireplace or red-ochre the doorstep if you did!

In the 1930s, there were times of individual personal tragedy in our families. An example was the time when Leonard, just two years old, lay dying of pneumonia in his hospital bed at St David's Hospital. His mother felt a pang of jealousy as she perceived his glance focussing upon his father, Walter. Yet, on further observation, she realised that his glance was toward the window. Leonard smiled. It was as if someone was beckoning him at the window. My brother died.

While our community had an ethos of interracial harmony and self-sufficiency in times of trials and tribulations (such as when my brother died), the *South Wales Echo* and the *Western Mail* had a rather different ethos. In the early 1930s, they began publishing excerpts from a study organised and designed to promote legislation to alter the conditions imposed upon coloured seamen throughout the country. These conditions were the result of a British racial policy that became more flagrant during the latter days of the British Empire.

In July of 1935, the following was published in the *Western Mail*:

> Hundreds of Arab and coloured seamen have settled in the city.... They construct their own places of worship.... They mate with the type of women who are willing to

accept them because there are none of their own kind to be had... The coloured men who have come to dwell in our cities are being made to adopt a standard of civilization they cannot be expected to understand....

There is no reason for sentimentality in this matter. Let him who pleads the justice of the coloured man's settlement among us read the report's references to venereal disease and the heavy toll of tuberculosis among our guests. Many of them are citizens of the British Empire; many did fine work in the war. Neither of these considerations should blind us to the plain fact that they do not belong to the social system we have evolved in these islands.

Despite the hard work my grandmother, Agnes Headley, had done for much of her life for the nuns in Penylan, in the "social system" mentioned above, she was merely one of "the type of women who are willing to accept" a black man. And, in that "system" her daughter, Beatrice, was referred to as a "half-caste."

Now, at a time before my brother Leonard died, Beatrice and her best friend Katie Nathan, two "half-caste" girls, decided on a day out uptown. They put on their best clothes to go. Of course, Leonard, who wasn't quite two, had to be taken along. There was rarely the convenience of babysitters back then in the 1930s, so babies were dressed up and taken too. Having spent a busy afternoon window-shopping and enjoying themselves, the thought of a nice "cup-a-tea" easily sprang to mind. So they stopped at an Italian cafe in St Mary's Street called Rabiotti.

They sat and they sat as waitresses continued to serve other customers, who came in after them. So Beatrice called for the manager, who promptly informed them that people like them could not be served there. Beatrice protested! She and her friend were tired and not leaving until they were served.

Here we have a mother, a child and her friend — all born in Wales — being "made to adopt a standard of civilization they cannot be expected to understand": they were politely escorted from the premises by a policeman the manager had contacted outside in St Mary's Street. The policeman explained it was the proprietor's prerogative if he chose not to serve them. So, in disgrace and indignation, they went without their tea.

This apparently was the enforcement of the policy that declared that people like Beatrice, Katie and poor little Leonard did not belong to "the social system we have evolved in these islands."

To maintain its barriers, the aforementioned "social system" forged the nomenclature "half-caste" out of Britain's experience as a dominating empire with its attendant colonial regime. Here we have a "standard of civilization" that refuses to accept the children it has made. The term "half-caste" is still used today in the media but it is not heard so much in Tiger Bay, as it was, up to the Black Consciousness movement of the 1960s.

"Half-caste" was a word I tended to hear more when I left the Bay to go to school in Bute Terrace. Pupils there from other parts of Cardiff more than once said to me:

"You're half-caste, ain't you?"

Cautiously, I'd say, "Yea... like, after all, what is it to you?"

Then, with my admission would come:

"Well, is your mother white?"

"No!" I'd say.

"So your father's white, then!"

"No!" again was my reply. Both my parents were "half-caste!"

Naturally, I personally could not feel comfortable with such a designation. After all, who is cast into this world? I was born. My parents were born. If labels must be placed, why "half-caste," that rather oddball term derived from a European colonialism and misguided, antiquated racialist philosophy about the alleged division of humanity.

There is no need for the continued usage of such an undignified term as "half-caste." It should be replaced by the complimentary terms of Afro-Celtic, Afro-Saxon, Indo-Cymric. These terms better represent our place in the capital city of modern Wales, which is why I began this story by praising 'the land of my mothers' rather than with 'the land of my fathers,' the traditional opening line of the Welsh National Anthem.

Evidence exists to indicate that this is not the first time we graced these shores. It appears that a Eurafrican Negroid human substratum existed in the Neolithic Age, as Alfred C Haddon states in his work, "The Races of Man and Their Distribution." This work shows that a 'brown race,' referred to as the 'Grimaldi' type, was found in "the Plynlimmon and other districts of south Wales...."[2] Geoffrey of Monmouth, in the Middle Ages, even believed that the original Welsh came from Troy — which, of course is in the east. Troy was a city much affected by the declining Ancient Egyptian civilisation long before its legendary contact with Ancient Greece. According to Geoffrey, the ancient Welsh were led by the mythical Brutus, whose son Camber was bequeathed the territory west of the Severn then known as Cambria. The people were called Cymry and spoke a language called Cymric.

Celtic heritage aside, when a person from Tiger Bay fills out an application for a job that includes an ethnic breakdown, he or she can, for all intents and purposes, practically say yes to every designated group! This phenomenon indicates that the time is long overdue for those born in Wales and with a Welsh matriarchal lineage to be recognised as Celtic, and for those with obvious African features to be recognised as Afro-Celtic. This determination would go without saying for the Indians,

Malays, Arabs and all the different nationalities that settled Old Tiger Bay and, of course, by extension for all ethnically intermixed communities throughout the rest of Britain — more assuredly for those of second and third generation. An end must be brought once and for all to the lack of acceptance implied in the term "half-caste." We are Welsh. Everything that happened to us, prior to and throughout this century, occurred in Wales. We are an indelible and recognisable part of Welsh history.

With what had been said before, St Mary's Street was becoming off-limits to people of colour, despite its close proximity to Tiger Bay and the fact that at that time the statue of the Marquis Bute faced in the direction of his beloved Docks. (For those interested or old enough to remember, his statue has spun on its axis a number of times since it was placed at the bottom of St Mary Street.)

Opposite the Italian cafe in St Mary's Street, which denied service to people of colour, was the Pavilion Cinema, where black beaux and their white lady friends spent many an evening at the pictures. However, this story isn't all one sided. White gents escorted their brown maidens too! It must be recalled Mr Blackman, a not so tall white gentlemen, came down to Maria Street smartly dressed, with his raincoat neatly placed over his right arm, to call upon his dark Venus. He stood in front of the door and knocked. When Lydia Hopkins opened the door, there he stood ready to escort her to the Pavilion.

"We can't go there!" she said.

"They're not letting black folks in any more!"

Aunty Annie Gordon, with her superlatively eloquent Welsh diction, couldn't go there with her black beau either! What was there to do? It was then, during the 1930s, that everyone down the Bay began to go to the Central Cinema on The Hayes, starting a tradition that was to continue on into the 1950s.

As the Day of Doom was approaching, the 1950s were to

bring an interesting turn of events for a City with a century-long tradition of "Colour Bar" as the only solution to "the problem" of its coloured folks down there by the sea!

The Pavilion Cinema, which once banned interracial couples in the 1930s, was now to be "shook, rattled and rolled" by the Black American music of Joe Turner — who appeared in the movie "Rock Around the Clock," singing the original verson of "Shake, Rattle & Roll." A song which was sung subsequently by Bill Haley and the Comets and various other white American and British artists. The movie "Rock Around the Clock" hailed in the Rock & Roll era in Great Britain.

The invasion of Rhythm & Blues and Rock & Roll were taking place as Cardiff City Planners were planning the destruction and uprooting of Tiger Bay. Most of the official studies and reports about our community published in the various newpapers of South Wales throughout the century left no doubt about the City's opinion of us as a community. Yet, with the events taking place, these notions were rapidly becoming outmoded.

In the hour of our doom, Marimba — the African ancestress, whose tears for the sorrow of her people, according to Bantu mythology, brought music to Earth to uplift their soul — sent forth music, originated in the American Deep South, that would influence the entire new "teenage" generation of British society as a whole. Albeit, that this music formed the background to the dismantling of Tiger Bay.

Once the trees were torn from their roots, Loudoun Square was the first part of Old Tiger Bay to undergo demolition. First two brown stone homes next to Netta Bispham's Shop ("Charlie's) had to be demolished on the southside in order to make an opening into Hodges Square, which was being built upon the filled in lock that once led from the Glamorganshire Canal to Old Hodges Row. On that same southside, toward the Canal end, there was an open space that led to the Canal. Some old cottages used to be there that had been damaged by the war. Those cottages formed a dangerous adventure playground for Tiger Bay children, which they called "Bombdies." Nevertheless, that derelict land in the corner of Loudoun Square was annually visited by the Gypsy Fair, usually in the autumn time. This event lit up our lives with its bright coloured lights, fair ground music, coconut shies, Noah's Ark and other rides and swings. Of course, this event, like Old Tiger Bay, was soon to be no more.

Shortly thereafter, the pylons were being pounded into what used to be the Park for the foundations of what were to be Loudoun House and Nelson House. Highrise buildings, the celebrated answer to the housing shortage in the 1960s, were planted in our park. Tiger Bay sympathises with other communities throughout Britain who suffered a similar fate.

On the day before her home in George Street was to be demolished, Josefina Hormachea removed all her valued possessions, then went back to her house and shop and gave it one final clean, sweeping the floors as though someone else was going to move in.

Many staunch old Tiger Bay families were moved from the area during that time and breaks in the continuity in the Tiger Bay lifestyle were beginning to rend the soul of the community. Disintegration of the social fabric was inevitable. Yet, even now, many struggle to maintain the old community integrity. The thought still occurs:

"Who was the unknown architect whose dream created our nightmare? If it ever should be known, would that it were possible to have him hung, drawn and quartered. Even the wrathful Hebrew God in all His mercy would find this punishment lenient."

But, alas, what is is what we have to contend with and Tiger Bay was reconstructed as a Cardiff City Council Estate with its official name of Bute Town. Well, it has been less than

30 years and the bright, new, shiny council homes are anything but these days. "The magic of Tiger Bay and the Docks has gone. Go behind into the vast colourless estate and you will find many nationalities and a community but essentially the heart is gone. It will never be regained...," stated Sue Richards of St Mary the Virgin Primary School in a Cardiff Bay Development Corporation project called, *Education Resource Pack*, published in 1987.

The "vast colourless estate," designed with anti-social lacklustre streets, is the more likely reason for the loss of heart in the current younger generation in Tiger Bay. The central focal point of our community, the park in Loudoun Square, has been destroyed. And the rows of streets, where front doors faced one another have been replaced with an architectural monstrosity that is not conducive to social harmony. Front doors now face the side or backs of other structures and do not form conventional streets. Furthermore, the anonymity of life in a block of flats adds to the disintegration of the community. Who will open their front door to an empty hallway? Who will take the time and pride to wash the stoop? How can you associate and congregate with your neighbour? The architecture clearly has had a profoundly destructive influence on such a once tightly knit society.

It is said that change is inevitable. However, it is not inevitably progressive. For example, when youngsters in Tiger Bay went to school from kindergarten to Secondary Modern the Tiger Bay community remained a close knit extended family. But nowadays youths go to Secondary Modern schools outside the area like Fitzalan and Bishop of Llandaff. They develop attachments and loyalties elsewhere, rendering tears in the fabric of our legendary togetherness.

It is known that in the aftermath of a nuclear catastrophe, Mother Nature recarpets the landscape with green grass, an abundance of flowers and small living creatures that survive unaffected by radiation. In the case of Tiger Bay, many people have survived unscathed but they, nonetheless, bear the mental scars caused by the devastation of a community and way of life seemingly gone forever.

Despite the despair and blight on the consciousness of a Tiger Bay generation that well remembers life before the devastation of the 1960s, you will find on any special occasion that the old Bay still gets together at the drop of a hat. At these events, you will see the past resurrected — old families reunited at reunions, funerals and weddings. They come from as far away as Germany, America, Canada — from anywhere from which they can get home.

It is at these events that a case can be made for the sacredness of the actual territory on which our community stands — the land once the pride of the Marquis of Bute. At these reunions a tremendous welling up of old passions and spirit is rekindled. The old music is played and great joy and mirth is displayed. Remember the 1982 Tiger Bay reunion? Prior to that occasion, the community had collected money so that events like bus trips and dances could be put on for those returning home to the reunion. Olwen Blackman Watkins had written to the proprietor of the Gordon Lennox Social Club, up the Valleys in the village near Aberfan, and asked, "Is there a welcome in the hillside?" so that the returnees could enjoy a truly Welsh night out! Of course, there was a welcome in the hillside, and a busload of Tiger Bay's temporary repatriates were whisked away to the Valleys. En route, Joanne Freeman said, "Look, isn't that where we used to go blackberry picking?" as she remembered, along with Shirley Caesaar, Deara Williams and many others, the time when they were evacuated as children during the war.

At the George Lennox Social Club it wasn't long before our local Tiger Bay talent were performing up on the stage. To the surprise of all the locals, Winnie Roberts did her superb rendition and interpretation of Ella Fitzgerald — and the crowd kept asking for more. Coming off the stage, Winnie said:

"What can I do next?"

The response was:

"Sing something in Welsh!" Which she did, beginning with "Sospan Fach." Winnie then sang on: you couldn't get her off the stage. The poor bus driver was quite peeved.

"Well," the situation was explained to him, "She was singing the Welsh National Anthem!"

"Yes," he said, "and everything else from Myfanwy to Cwm Rhondda!!!"

On tours further afield, such as the 1982 reunion group's trip to London, things seemed to change somewhat. Once the group dispersed into the anonymity of the big city, the shared sense of joy became less effusive. It seems that once away from Tiger Bay and things Welsh, the togetherness diminishes. Perhaps it is the actual standing upon our own "sacred territory" that, in fact, accentuates the spirit of togetherness, so legendary to the community of Tiger Bay.

Chapter Eight

THE LEGEND, THE MEDIA AND TIGER BAY

For generations journalists and academics have been giving us "authoritative" accounts of what life was like in the heyday of Tiger Bay. Most of these accounts confuse fact with fiction. Take for example the professor from Swansea University, who has recently been portrayed as an "expert" on our community. According to a report in the *South Wales Echo* in the spring of 1992, the professor's research uncovered the "fact" that Tiger Bay once had 300 houses of ill-repute and 500 prostitutes. Now, why should anyone believe his findings, unless they are based upon his own experiences of frequenting such houses and seeking the services of all 500!

People born in Tiger Bay at the turn of the century do not agree that this level of vice existed in the community in their lifetime. So if the professor's claims are true, his period would have been some time between the establishment of the area in the 1840s and the end of the previous century, which is odd, when you consider that during that time period, this area housed the height of Cardiff's bourgoise society and was the richest part of Cardiff until money went uptown. Old Loudoun Square had some stately homes and the private garden of the Marquis of Bute [in Mount Stuart Square] was, presumably, amongst the residences where the ladies of the night allegedly plied their trade.

Once again, we in Tiger Bay have been subjected to the psychosexual fantasies of the media, which seems to delight in regurgitating stories of vice and corruption supposedly typical of world seaport communities and, therefore, easily foisted onto the Tiger Bay legend.

Many a young man from sea or valley found himself

beaten up in Old Bute Street, after having gone into a pub and asking the first woman he saw, "How much for a good time, dear?" only to discover the woman in question was a respectable wife!

Yes, our community is subject to the foibles of the human race. There were prostitutes in Tiger Bay, just as you would find in any city, or for that matter in other parts of Cardiff. But, when I was a child in the 1940s and 1950s, I do not recall being overwhelmed by such activity. However, there was an incident that still stands out in my mind.

For years, directly opposite my home in Frances Street, lived a white family, the Yarwoods. Angela Yarwood and I had become fast friends by the time her family moved away from Tiger Bay altogether. Their house, at number 6, was not unoccupied for long, as some rather over-dressed and made-up ladies soon moved in.

Although our street was predominantly one of family homes, no one seemed to take offence to the newcomers, who had a stream of strange men frequently visiting the house. No adult discussed the goings on at this house in front of me. However, on one rather overcast day, a black maria pulled up in front. Soon all the neighbours from Frances Street and Old Angelina Street and some from Sophia Street had gathered around in a semi-circle to see what was going on. Mrs Evora stood tiptoe in the back of the crowd. And Johnnie Lima and I watched as the police trundled the ladies and some of their gents into the back of the black maria never to be seen again!

This was my first knowledge of the existence of such places as brothels — and so close to home! Yet, like many other locals, I was fascinated by those well-dressed ladies, who spoke with London accents, which were so rare to hear in Tiger Bay. [It was only much later in life, and with much amusement, that my mother related to me of the time two Japanese gentlemen knocked our front door in search of the special services that were to be found at no. 6. As they were looking for a house with a blue door - ours was green — Mam redirected them to the opposite side of the street.]

Not long after the aforementioned scandal, the Yarwood's old house became a boarding house for Arab seamen. Apart from the fact that they were often seen holding hands — which is customary in the Middle East and Africa — all the scandalous excitement died down and life went back to normal.

When I was of sufficient age to be aware of the seedier side of life (in the 1950s), I seem to remember that it was WESTGATE STREET [in the centre of town] which was notorious for prostitution. The well-groomed ladies of Westgate Street were quite a sight to behold!

To youngsters in the real Tiger Bay, all adults were "uncle" or "aunty" — including some prostitutes.

One who might nowadays have been considered notorious was a madam named "Sadie." Although she came from the East End of London, and had a strong East End accent, Sadie was definitely a part of the Tiger Bay scene — because of her association with people in the community since World War II. Despite being quite overweight, she was always well-groomed and a remarkable dancer. Although she did run a house of ill-repute, Sadie also had a legitimate restaurant in Bute Terrace, where she employed many local people at one time or another.

Clearly, the fact that there were as many churches, chapels, mosques and missions in Tiger Bay as there were pubs adds little spice to the historical record. Who is interested in knowing that entire families in the "urban village" of Tiger Bay frequented these places of worship?

Who is interested to recall the Ebenezer Chapel in Mount Stuart Square, where we said our last goodbye to our friend, Maxine Reese? I recall Maxine, with her blond kinky hair, riding her bicycle up and down Old Angelina Street, near where her grandmother lived, before that fateful day an accident on that very bike took her away. The Ebenezar Chapel underwent a transformation in the 1950s, when it became the Seven Arts nighclub and later The Metropole. (More recently it became the Casablanca.)

The fact is vice and corruption in Tiger Bay were minimal compared with any other part of Cardiff or any major capital in the world, unless you refer to illegal gambling as vice. Men of all nationalities gambled openly on that corner in front of Kerrigan's Marchioness of Bute while others stood around chatting. Was this vice? Nobody living here thought so.

Nevertheless, in the spring of 1993, on the 4th of May, to be exact, *The Independent*, together with other national newspapers, television and radio, were broadcasting that Tiger Bay was the location of Cardiff's "flourishing community of prostitutes." The story infuriated the many decent members of the community, especially since not one of the "12 members of the city's flourishing community of prostitutes," mentioned in this report, came from Tiger Bay.

Such slander has a long history. Another recent example comes from a *South Wales Echo* reporter, who quotes an anonymous source, claiming that the drug ghat has created devastation in the "Arab" community of Cardiff. For those who do not know, ghat is a legally available vegetable-based stimulant substance, which people of the Middle East and North Africa have traditionally used. It is much like chewing tobacco.

Arabs have lived in Tiger Bay since its legendary beginnings. There is no doubt that people in this world suffer from one drug problem or another, but where are the crazed and frenzied Arab drug addicts in Tiger Bay? I see the Somalies purchasing ghat out of the back of the ghat man's car in as orderly as manner as the crowds who buy ice cream and cockles or rent videos from street vendors.

On 14th June 1993, we were yet again treated to media

vitriolic when *The Independent* made reference to the dreadful beating to death of a resident of the Ely Housing Estate in the west of Cardiff. Reporter Andrew Gliniecki, who apparently simply could not resist including a mention of Tiger Bay, stated that in Ely, "Many of the families were moved from the Tiger Bay area of the city's docklands." Perhaps we are to understand that this horrendous crime would not have occurred had those families not moved to Ely in the 1960s!

The one fact missing from all this negative publicity involving Tiger Bay is that it has the lowest overall crime rate in the city of Cardiff. Home insurance is also lower than anywhere else in the city, because of the low incidence of burglarisation of homes.

So, once again, we have outside media imposing onto Tiger Bay the problems of the world. The world should only be so lucky to enjoy the way people of Tiger Bay traditionally treat one another and come to each other's aid in times of crisis, no matter what their ethnic background or sexual persuasion. Many a benefit dance has been held in the Butetown Community Centre on behalf of members of the community who are in crisis.

We cannot permit this casting of negative aspersions onto our community by the media without comment. In a bizarre but fortuitous way, such negative publicity has served in the past to keep our community somewhat isolated and protected from those who believed the myths but feared to come and discover the truth. These are the people who continue to write about us in a derogatory way.

All those who know the real Tiger Bay know how it actually is here — and the true legend or our community still lives!

Chapter Nine

THE TIGER'S YOUTH

We are grateful to all those who endeavoured over the years to improve the lives and prospects of the youth of our community. We recall with affection Mr Iorwerth John, who started the Play Centre in Bute Street; Donald Andrews, who ran the Neptune Club in Bute Street, just north of Old Maria Street; Pastor Wright of the Mission in Old Angelina Street; Mrs Capener of the Rainbow Club, also in Bute Street; and the Park Keeper ("Parkee" to us). We are grateful to them and to all those others who endeavoured to raise our sights and in the process became part of the Tiger Bay family.

Because the Second World War prevented the youth of the community from having holidays away at the seaside, Loudoun Square Park was declared a playground for the benefit of local children. A paddling pool, swings, a seesaw, and a slide were provided for that purpose. This community can

On the left, just past Mahfud's cafe, is Mrs Capener's Rainbow Club at the top of the bridge in Bute Street, leaving Tiger Bay for town. Now replaced by Callaghan Square, this is also the same bridge where police once warned rioters in 1919 to venture into Tiger Bay at their own peril.

St Mary's Primary School at the corner of North Church Street and Bute Street. At this school, Miss King was Headmistress to many generations of children from Tiger Bay.

only applaud these efforts. Nevertheless, we have been and, on occasion continue to be, treated like a colonial possession. Conscious of our identity with Patrice Lumumba, Jomo Kenyatta and Kwame Nkrumah, an anti-colonial movement was formed in Tiger Bay in the 1950s. Benno Johnson opened the Ghana Club in honour of Kwame Nkrumah's effort in the decolonisation of the Gold Coast in 1957. However, we also recall the various heads of local community centres, where many times ex-colonial types, used to "dealing" with colonial subjects, were commissioned to work in Tiger Bay, as if it was actually a colony within Europe. In some quarters, this attitude continues and needs to be addressed.

As for school I, like so many of the youth in Tiger Bay, attended the Old St Mary's School that once stood on the corner of Bute Street and North Church Street, where now stands the PDSA, a veterinary clinic. Miss King, who was Headmistress then, saw to the education of several generations in Tiger Bay. However, after all her strivings, if you didn't pass the 11-Plus examination, the only Secondary Modern options available were the Board School in South Church Street or St Mary's Bute Terrace. Of course, St Cuthbert's Primary School provided education for those of the Catholic faith but, nevertheless, in our multi-religious community, we all found ourselves in each other's places of worship at one time or another.

So, although there were few opportunities available to Tiger Bay youth outside the community at that time, one could get a complete education without leaving the area's confines. Alas, this is not true today. Youngsters have the option of three primary schools: St Cuthbert's, St Mary's; and Mount Stuart (of which Ms Betty Campbell, MBE, is current Head Teacher — the first Black women in Wales to hold such a position.) However, no facility for secondary education exists since the demolition of the Board School in the early 1960s. At their most critical age, the youth of Tiger Bay are exported to Grange Council, Bishop of Llandaff, Fitzalan and other institutions outside the community. The result has been the further deterioration of the continuity of old Tiger Bay's extended family tradition. As our youth "widen their horizons" and form alliances and loyalties outside the community, there is a corroding of the sense of togetherness and responsibility that used to exist in a bygone time. One does not hear, "We are the Boys from Tiger Bay," sung anymore.

Mr Sheskonas was Headmaster of South Church Street School, known to all as the "Board School." He was a great lover of motorcycles and was a champion cross-country motocycle rider. As its headmaster, he was often likened by his his pupils to Hitler, because of his severity and even more so for his bald head and rimless glasses, which made him appear like Erich von Stroheim, the stereotypical Hollywood Nazi. Yet, it was the teachers, under his administration, that educated generations of families in Tiger Bay. Teachers like Peter Cronin and Bernard Sullivan had an endearing love of the community and did their utmost to insure that many graduated with an actual education.

Prior to teaching at the Education Board School, Mr Sullivan had served his time in the Royal Air Force. When he

The Educational Board School or, as we knew it, South Church Street School, before demolition (circa 1963).

began to teach at Tiger Bay's main school, prior to Secondary Modern School days, its reputation for being tough had preceded it, so he prepared himself in advance to handle what he believed would be a difficult assignment.

According to Olwen Blackman, who was one of the pupils in his first class, Mr Sullivan entered the room like James Cagney, tossing a piece of chalk up in the air, as he leaned nonchalantly against the classroom wall.

"I've heard about how tough you are all supposed to be so I'm letting you know I've just come out of the Air Force and have fought this country's deadliest enemies. So don't think you're going to get away with anything with me!" said he.

"Hark at him in his blue chalk stripped demob suit going on about how tough he is!" exclaimed Gloria Erskine, amid the roaring laughter of the entire class. It seemed, from that moment on, he graciously yielded to the acknowledgement that he might as well give up the tough guy image, as he didn't stand a chance.

There before him was a field of bright, alert, young minds with great potential, if only it was cultivated properly. And that is what he set out to do.

Nicknamed "Bunny," Mr Sullivan was a good sport, who recognised that talent was going to waste here and so he set about expanding this charge's horizons. He imposed homework on his pupils, who heretofore had never been assigned such tasks.

It was Mr Sullivan who, through his dedication, brought Shakespeare to Standard Three in the 1950s. Under his tutelage, the class put on a first rate performance of "A Midsummer Night's Dream" and a stunning performance of "The Merchant of Venice." In the latter production, Norman "Sweet" Dowbella of Canal Parade played "Shylock."

Coming from a family of Anglo-Arabic origin, poor Norman was to catch hell after the performance, when his Arab father discovered his son was playing a Jew! Also in this play, Ronald Sinclair, "Sinkie" to his friends, played "Bassanio."

"A Midsummer Night's Dream," the 1950 production of Shakespeare's play, by South Church Street School. Left to right: Ronald Sinclair, Geraldine Grant, Said Mohammed and Amadora Papadatos.

Said "Cider," Mohammed, from a Malay family of Old Nelson Street, played "Antonio," while Patti Young, now known as the cabaret star "Patti Flynn," played "Portia."

With the permission of their parents, the entire cast studied their lines at Mr Sullivan's home in Splott and his wife always provided the necessary tea and cakes.

A scene from the aforementioned play was on the front page of the *South Wales Echo* at the time. Other photographs abound in many households of Tiger Bay of that proud occasion to this very day.

At the 1982 Tiger Bay Reunion, Mr Sullivan was to be guest of honour but, unfortunately, he died a week prior to the occasion.

Ronald Sinclair became an all-round sportman under the

1951 South Church Street Rugby Team. From top row left to right: Conrad Hutchins, Phillip Celia, Siddie Nogan, Jack Atard, Roy Abookie, Donnie Graham, Mr. Stainer, Ray Silva, Unknown, Royston Whiteman, Mr. Evans, Raymond Fettah, Brian Actie, Karim Mohammed, Philpot Williams, Ronald Sinclair, Herbert Boston and Grenville.

tutelage of his school, excelling in swimming, boxing, rugby and cricket. He had a personality that endeared him to the entire community. Ronnie's friend, Norman Dowbella, recalls him as a natural athlete, when both he and Ronnie swam for Cardiff at that time. Ronnie and Norman belonged to the 12th Cardiff Scout Troop, which held their meetings in the old Vestry of the Church of St Mary. Ronnie was Patrol Leader of the Bulldog Patrol, while Billy Miller of Loudoun Square was flag bearer. All this activity was under the watchful eye of Father Garland, who had been the community priest since 1928.

At the Neptune Club, run by Donald Andrews, Ronald built a canoe, which he raced on the West Junction Canal. The

Ronald Sinclair (centre) and other members of the Neptune Club building the canoe he raced. In the centre is youth worker, Shiela More, giving some helpful instructions.

Neptune Club was in Bute Street, on the same block as the Maria Street Police Station. It was a youth centre sponsored by Save The Children Fund. I remember being on the bridge that crossed the West Junction Canal, near the old Salvation Army building, watching the canoes race toward and under the bridge with everyone cheering Ronnie on.

But there were few, if any, real opportunities offered to youth from Tiger Bay. Thus, young men like Ronald still looked to the sea for a career: becoming a sea cadet became his sole ambition. Eventually, he followed in his forefather's footsteps and took to the sea. Tragedy struck on his second voyage, while sailing in the Indian Ocean where, it was said, he fell into an empty cargo hold, breaking his neck. It was said he was still alive when brought up to deck.

As no refrigeration to speak of existed on ships during the 1950s, Ronald was given a sea burial and never returned to Tiger Bay, much to the heartbreak of his family and the entire community. For his memorial service, the Board School closed and everyone attended his service at St Mary the Virgin. While I stood in my church pew, the whole congregation sang J B Dyker's "Eternal Father of the Sea" — which has rung in my ears ever since.

I was about 10 years old at the time and remember the knock on the front door while my mother, father, sister and I were having a midday dinner. I left the dinner table, closing the living room door behind me. In the frame of our front door, standing next to his bicycle, was a man in a gabardine raincoat, wearing a tribly style hat.

"Is your father home, son?" he asked and I went back to the dinner table saying:

It's for you, Dad."

Dad went to the door and we continued to eat.

As time progressed, my mother became alarmed and went to the passage. There, as she opend the door, I could see

Walter and Beatrice Sinclair with the Ronald Sinclair memorial Cup in 1954.

my father convulsing in tears on his knees. While mother tried to ascertain what was wrong, she kept saying:

It's Ronnie. Dear God, it's Ronnie!"

Life has never been the same for me since then. Shortly after this tragedy, the family decided to leave Ronald a memorial and the Ronald Sinclair Cup, presented annually by the Cardiff Schools Rugby Club, came into existence at that time. Many times over the years, this cup has been presented by Ronnie's teacher, Peter Cronin.

Tragedy comes, but eventually laughter returns. Worshipping God and attending funerals were not the only purpose the community had for church pews. Church pews from St Mary's Church were often put on the backs of lorries so that Tiger Bay families could have a day away on a farm as a Whitsun treat. Look out countryside, here we come!

Left to right: Peter "Pepsi" Findlayson, me as a child, and Ronnie on an outing to Swanbridge. Little companion with Ronnie unknown.

At the end of a tiring day, we would load onto the back of the lorries, Father Oman and all, and make our way back home to Tiger Bay. As the lorries passed the Marquis of Bute's statue at the bottom of St Mary Street, all on board would start to sing:

"Here we are! Here we are! Here we are, again! Hello! Hello! Hellohelohelo!"

Of course, doors opened and curtains moved as we drove to West Church Street to disembark and be greeted by the rather dark-skinned Father Cannon Quati, our visiting clergyman from Ghana.

With sadness, one realises that Tiger Bay is a ghost of its former self. Nevertheless, the many people referred to in this book still live and there is still a resilience to be found in their young descendants. There is Linda Mitchell, for one. A Tiger Bay girl, who has become quite a television celebrity. The family of her grandfather, Mr Abdullah, was in Maria Street, opposite the Britos and the Pines. Her mother Zaneb was one of many including Miriam, Cassim and Hussein. Mr Abdullah also owned a cafe in Maria Street, poised at the head of Angelina Street commanding a panoramic view all the way down to Loudoun Square. Steve Mitchell, her father, along with Benjamin Ritchie, arrived in Tiger Bay from Jamaica after disembarking from the *SS Empire Windrush* in the late 1940s. When I played with her uncle, Hussein, he used to take me to his father's cafe and I can still recall the spotless white tiles that went halfway up and around all the walls, which surrounded the older Arab men, who played cards and drank coffee.

There is, of course, Shirley Bassey, an international star, who has contributed to the fame of Tiger Bay throughout the world. Unfortunately, her relationship with the community itself is quite sour. Yet, despite Shirley Bassey's defection from her native community and rebuff of many of her childhood friends, she is still part of what made Tiger Bay. And she has a right to live in Europe in self-exile in her own self-made glory!

Marcia Brahim recalls the Mbakwe family of Old Evelyn Street, especially the day all the children had been given new bicycles. They rode them in circles near their house, which was right next door to the Empress Eugene pub. It seemed they dared anyone to bother them on their bikes, while Jeremiah, there father, stood in the doorway, in this white singlet snug fit over his dark-skinned torso, arms akimbo, displaying great pride in this children. "Chuku," the name given to the power most high by the Igbo of West Africa, was given as a name to his second son. His eldest boy, he named after himself. Both the brothers have grown up to become world class champions in Karate and they still train and teach in Cardiff today.

Leonora Brito, a descendant of the Lima family of Old Frances Street, has recently become an acclaimed writer. Who knows what her pen will reveal in years to come?

Obviously, the potential talent yet to come from Tiger Bay is still being nurtured, despite an encroaching disintegration.

Chapter Ten

THE TIGER GROWLS

As a result of ostracism, racism and other trials and tribulations, the community consciousness has risen. We are fighting the good fight. Only the other day, I heard retold of the good work of Flori Fernandez, Renee (Hinds) Phillips, and Mrs Trotman, and others in the local Labour Party back in the 1940s.

In the heyday of Flori Fernandez' all-woman local Labour Party activity, James Callaghan was our local MP. On one occasion in the 1940s, Mr Callaghan took a group of South Church Street School pupils to London to see the workings of the Houses of Parliament. The group included Peter McCarthy,

South Church Street School on a trip to the Houses of Parliament with teacher, Bernard Sullivan and our then MP and future Prime Minister, Lord James Callaghan. In the centre, and to the far left, is my uncle and aunt, Jackie and Helen Sinclair, respectively. Among the others present are: Veronica Musa, Louis Brito, Peter McCarthy, Teddy Ali, Johnny Freeman, Joey Erskine, Georgie 'Sultana' Ahmed, Freddie Summers, David Saleh, Maureen Jemmett, Mary Jones, Terry Fettah, Margaret Ali, Rosie Rafur, Dorothy Beddoes and Shirley Hassan.

Jackie and Helen Sinclair, to name a few. On that occasion, at the age of 15, Helen Sinclair recalled her first realisation of racial prejudice in Britain, when she saw "Blackie Go Home!" written in large letters upon a wall.

Mr Callaghan was a regular visitor to the homes of Tiger Bay, where he was offered and drank many a cup-a-tea.

The work of the local Labour Party continued to operate even after the demolition of Tiger Bay in the 1960s. However, as the members, by then, were mainly senior citizens, their activities evolved into a social club in the Butetown Community Centre, as the main political stalwarts, like Flori Fernandez and her fellow colleagues, had long passed away.

In the old days, the "Sons of Africa" held their meetings in the "George Cross Community Centre" in Bute Street, near Old Sophia Street. Who were more dignified than the old Africans of Tiger Bay, who always doffed their hat to a gentleman or lady? We of Tiger Bay know what the UN is trying to achieve: never forget that we lived it!

Since the rise of organisations such as the Commission for Racial Equality, pride in the Tiger Bay community is beginning to express itself in the form of legal action. Thus, it was great to see the smiling face of "Liz" (Elizabeth Musa) but sad to see she lost her case. Or had she? Liz did what many more of us should do and we of Tiger Bay must applaud her effort for advancing the way. She brought a case of racial discrimination against the Cardiff City Council because she was more than qualified for a position she was later denied. Now, we all have heard various organisations claim they want to hire people from the local community, and they certainly do a great public relations job for themselves in this regard, but when the dirt settles from the stampede of applications, it is people from outside the community that get the responsible jobs.

Many times the claim has been made that one can't find qualified people in the community, yet we know this is not true.

In the early 1990s, Henrietta Neil, highly qualified and college educated, left for London, after expending a great deal of effort to be employed nearer home. Around the same time, Betty Farrah's son, Ibrahim Hassan, also left home to find work in computer science. This sort thing has been going on for generations. I, myself, left Tiger Bay in the early sixties to find "fame and fortune" owing to lack of opportunity for us in Tiger Bay. Moreover, efforts are made to train those who do not have the required skills and yet afterwards they are still not employed and in Tiger Bay and the Docks this doesn't just apply to those of us of African descent, it applies to all of us who live here. Though to be fair, some have been employed, especially in the construction field.

Beside the disadvantage of "colour," the prejudice of location can be equally damaging. For generations local people would not be hired if their applications showed that they were from the Tiger Bay area. This practice often continues today. Proving the point, of course, is next to impossible. It is just a factor with which we in Tiger Bay have had to deal. Even if one looked Caucasian, an Arabic or African surname could betray your ethnic origin where employment was concerned.

Returning to the case of Liz Musa, on the day of the Tribunal, a representative of Equal Opportunities for Cardiff City Council was asked if equal opportunities were working and he declared that they were not at that time. However, new procedures have been set in place as management level members have been attending "three-day courses" on equal opportunity awareness — this during and subsequent to Liz's complaint.

Liz did not feel bitter in the least but felt she had to bring this case forward for those who come after her. She lost the battle but not the war as Cardiff City Council changed much of its interviewing technique and now advertises that it is "striving to be an equal opportunity employer."

Well, we take our hats off to Liz and hope that the local authorities and the various new companies emerging in and around Tiger Bay mean what they say about assisting the community and do not let us down this time, because we want them to know we are prepared to struggle not to be overlooked. Especially since a far more serious miscarriage of justice occurred to residents in the community in the late 1980s — the now well-known case of THE CARDIFF THREE, which is the subject of the following chapter.

Chapter Eleven

VOICE OF THE TIGER

When I saw Los Angeles burning in May of 1992, I was not the least surprised. I say this as an Afro-Celtic observer, having lived in LA for the last 12 years. It is true I returned home to be closer to my family, but I was also discontented with the rise of hostile behaviour I was experiencing living there, close friends excepted.

The latest miscarriage of justice in the Western Judicial System involving the Rodney King incident was merely the catalyst, the proverbial "straw that broke the camel's back," igniting the heat that I felt building while living there. It should be noted that these developments arose under the Reagan/ Thatcher/Bush administrations. There is a connection here.

Thank God that Watts stood up as the "conscience" of the United States of America. No matter what the cost of the damage caused by such uninhibited rioting and the unfortunate consequent loss of lives, what we saw was rage against the injustices faced by the poor.

Which brings us closer to home. The Cardiff Three, wrongly imprisoned for the murder of Lynette White, suffered a profound miscarriage of justice.

During the month of May, Tony Parris had been returned to Cardiff Jail and local people and friends and family had an opportunity to visit him and show him their support and support for the entire case. When I saw Tony, he was looking well and keeping his spirits intact by involving himself in arts and crafts and drama classes.

He had developed a strong sense of concern for other prisoners he is convinced have also been wrongly convicted.

He thanked his family and the community from the bottom of his heart for the support shown for The Cardiff Three in its campaign for justice.

As a community, we still demand justice for Lynette White but we also want justice for The Cardiff Three. We also felt that the media should retract the prosecution's dreadful and ill-informed description of people living in Tiger Bay as some form of knife carrying night creatures living in a "topsy turvy" world.

The stituation is not as socially chronic in Britain as it is in the USA, but nontheless multiple miscarriages of justice have occurred. So many families were affected by the case of The Cardiff Three as prior to their conviction many more young men were detained or held under suspicion. Because Tiger Bay is an extended family type of community, the entire community in essence was under suspicion. The Acties, Trotmans, Rodericks, Grahams, Sinclairs, Davids, Bostons, Wilsons and Erkines are some of the oldest and well-respected "royal" families of Tiger Bay.

Even today the spirit of community togetherness is still finding its expression in the younger generations: they rallied to defend the honour and dignity of those wrongly accused and convicted; and desire to see justice prevail in the case of young Lynette. This is the spark that continues to light the way for the future of Tiger Bay.

On Saturday, 23rd November 1991, the controversial Reverend Al Sharpton came to the Tiger Bay community prepared to march with the locals in protest against the arrest and conviction of the three for the brutal and sadomasochistic murder of Lynette White. The Reverend's visit was preceded by a lot of media hype concerning his alleged racism and provocation to violence.

A press conference, organised by the National Black Caucus, took place at the Big Windsor Hotel in Stuart Street prior to the march. A wide spectrum of the media were represented, including the *Daily Telegraph*, *The Observer* and the BBC, among others. Some members of the press expressed concern about potential violence erupting but were informed that local people here are like an extended family, all interrelated and descended from a long local history of legendary togetherness.

Nevertheless, there was a great deal of division in the community regarding whether "The Boys," who had been convicted, could commit such a horrendous crime. Listening to opinions from all sides I, too, had become naturally ambivalent. In such an atmosphere, one had to ask "Are they innocent?" However, upon deeper reflection, our subjective opinions were formed without access to forensic evidence and as such lacked foundation. Thus, the issue was: Did the forensic evidence indicate beyond a shadow of a doubt that "The Cardiff Three" committed this crime or not?

At the conference table, Reverend Sharpton was flanked on his left by Mrs Pauline Abdullahi, mother of Yusef Abdullahi; and on his right by both Malik Abdullahi, Yusef's brother, and Lloyd Parris, brother of Anthony "Tony" Parris. Yusef and Tony were the two local boys convicted for this murder. One member of The Cardiff Three, Stephen Miller, came from London and did not grow up in the Bay. Given the controversy that preceded him, I was perplexed to know exactly how Reverend Sharpton would benefit the Tiger Bay community in this matter. However, under questioning by the media, Reverend Sharton elaborated that his attorneys in the United States had reviewed the legal transcripts of this trial and the evidence upon which The Cardiff Three were convicted. His legal staff had concluded that a miscarriage of justice had apparently occurred. Furthermore, he stated that the interests of justice could be furthered if in the western world persons of colour were tried in courts by multiracial juries.

In the community there was an ardent belief that The Cardiff Three were the victims of a political frame-up. It is believed that the local police constabulary were put under pressure to resolve this case as quickly as possible in the interest of economic concerns regarding the redevelopment occurring in the area.

Most people familiar with "The Boys" were well-aware that these three lads belonged to three different "posses." They moved in completely different circles and, that being the case, why would they join together on this one occasion to commit such an obscene crime?

Be that as it may, following the press conference, hundreds marched along Bute Street through Tiger Bay and on to the Law Courts in the City Centre. En route, the procession stopped in front of Cardiff Prison demonstrating a show of support for Yusef Abdullahi, one of The Cardiff Three, who had been temporarily returned there. From the steps of the Law Courts several thought-provoking speeches were delivered and when he spoke Reverend Sharpton was warmly received by the crowd. Yet *The Observer* merely described the event in a one inch column as a "noisy but peaceful march." Perhaps, had there been a riot there would have been no end of publicity.

Subsequently, in fairness to the media, the television programme, "Week In, Week Out," broadcast in South Wales in early January 1991, emphasised the lack of connection between the forensic evidence and the men who were convicted. And more encouragingly, the appeals of Tony, Yusef and Stephen Miller were set to be heard in December 1992.

Not long after the aforementioned broadcast, the same issue casting doubt about the lack of forensic evidence was once again emphasised on "Panorama" by the BBC.

Toward the end of the summer of 1992, the mother of Lynette White was reported to say in the *South Wales Echo* that she did not believe that the right people had been convicted of her daugher's murder.

"Are Our Boys guilty?" was the question asked before the Appeal Court quashed their convictions at the December 1992 Hearing. [In 2002, genetic tests also eliminated them from suspicion.] The people of Tiger Bay would like to see justice done, not least on behalf of Lynette White. The case should be reopened to find the man with blood on his hands, originally under suspicion, and to arrest, try and, if guilty, convict him. Then we could all sleep more soundly.

With demonstrations supported by the Socialist Worker's Party and through the effort of Malik Abdullahi and Lloyd Parris, brothers of two of the convicted, national and international attention was brought to this case.

Chapter Twelve

TIGER BAY — IS THERE A FUTURE?

The murmuring and rippling sound of the tide, gently coming into the Bay, is soon to become a past memory, like the life that once vitalised the effervescent community of Tiger Bay. It is more than likely that Cardiff Bay Development Corporation will succeed in creating a lake at the shorefront of Cardiff City, leaving the tide to ebb outside the confines of a magnificant tidal-resisting Barrage.

Many days have I sat at the edge of this bay imbibing the refreshing sound of the sea, seeking solace and inspiration for many of the images recalled in the pages of this book. I think I shall miss that soft caressing sound in the bay, as much as I miss the Tiger Bay that can no longer be.

It seems there will be no more seamen, adding excitement to a Saturday night, spending their money in Old James Street in the pubs and nightclubs so popular until the 1950s and early 1960s. Take, for example, the North Star Club, the haunt of many a Scaninavian seafarer in the days when it was located upstairs at the corner of Louisa Street, on the same side as the Boilermakers Club and the Docks Non-Political Club.

Across the street, and opposite the Non-Political Club, was the Ship & Pilot, which, since then, has seen many a landlord. And, opposite that establishemnt, in Mount Stuart Square, you could find the entrance to the Oasis Club. Once inside the door, a metal trellised gate opened into a tiny lift, which allowed only four very slim people to enter. Always a sense of fear presided in the claustrophobic interior, as you were whisked up to the top floor into one of Cardiff's more exciting venues. Live jazz, as well as the best in American popular music, with the essential Calypsos and Cha Cha thrown in, you would get for your ten shilling entrance fee. I always wonder what would have happened if a fire broke out with only one tiny lift available to reach safety.

A little walk further down James Street, toward the Dock Gate entrance and above the Bombay Restaurant, which was always crowded when the clubs and pubs had closed, was the very popular Top Floor Club. I was really too young in those days to be let in, but I simply had to get in the night I was walking down the incline of West Bute Street and heard the voice of Ray Charles for the very first time singing "What'd I Say," along with the sound of the crowd revelling inside. It's a wonder the floor of the Top Floor Club didn't cave in, the way the Bay Folk used to like to stomp in those days.

When the Top Floor Club closed, it wasn't long before the Club 12 opened, just around the corner in James Street, directly facing George Street. So many nights, I spent dancing to the Club 12 juke box, and it was especially hot on the weekends that the GIs would come into town bringing all the steps to the latest dance crazes. Besides the obligatory "Jive," the "Slop" was the favourite and every now and then folks would break into the "Chicken."

At the other end of George Street, running parallel with James Street, was Stuart Street. In the early 1960s, Tom Jones sang for pints of beer in the Little Windsor (opposite the Big Windsor) — as Mary Fletcher, who was barmaid at that time, recalls. Around the corner on Bute Street was Cyril Clarke's first night club venture, The Colony Club, from which Tom Jones was unceremoniously turned away, due to his rowdy reputation. Of course, he wasn't known by this stage name of Tom Jones then.

Today, subsequent to the demolition of George, Louisa, South William, Evelyn and Adelaide Streets, each with busy little shops located on their corners, James Street is a mere shadow of its former self. Rarely will you find Saturday night revellers there now.

There again, life in Tiger Bay was never only a party. There was always the mundane side of life to take care of — sending the kids to school, tending the garden, buying what you needed. When you wanted fresh fish and didn't have money to pay, Tom-The-Fish would give it to you "on the tick." If you couldn't wait for the insurance man to come, his money could be left on the front room or kitchen table, as Maudrina Fettah of Nelson Street often did. And, incidentally, nothing but the money was taken while the house was empty and the front door ajar.

Since the loss of Loudoun Square as a main community focal point for meeting, greeting and seeing the world go by, many have wondered if, perhaps, West Close could take its place. Since the 1940s, there has been an unattractive concrete circle in the midst of otherwise rather nice homes. The ancient trees, uprooted from the Old Loudoun Square, could find a welcome home in West Close, with the addition of green grass and perhaps flower beds. Of course, benches would be necessary for the elderly to pass the time away or watch the rest of the local inhabitants. There needs to be an outside place for the elderly — like the old Tiger Bay men who used to sit on the park wall in Old Loudoun Square, scouring the newspaper for the best horse to bet on (and who refused to move when film director J Lee Thompson wanted to film a deserted Loudoun Square in a scene from the movie, "Tiger Bay").

Today, "The Bay," as Bute Town is still referred to by its inhabitants, has now found a much wider recognition. Old Tiger Bay is now completely surrounded by the martime regeneration undertaken by Cardiff Bay Development Corporation. "The Bay" has expanded to cover 2,700 acres of South Cardiff. Yet, even though this term refers to the actual bay created under the leadership of the Marquis of Bute, it still cannot dissociate itself from the history of Tiger Bay in Wales. After all, was it not the Portuguese seamen who thought the bay was like a bay of tigers?

At its beginning, this bay beckoned Black, Brown and Yellow seamen to its shores. The black seamen, who sang their calypso, "It was on St David's Day that we docked in Tiger Bay...," were soon to come into contact with the coal-blackened faces of Welshmen from the Valleys. Together they worked for the benefit and glory of a venture, conceived by the Marquis of Bute, that was to turn a small almost rural village into the Capital City of Wales.

However, over the sweep of this entire century, the inhabitants of Tiger Bay have seen an army of missionaries, in one form or another, march into the community with the purpose of improving or changing our community ways, alleged by mythology to be degenerate. They still come.

More often than not, these well-intentioned liberals come armed with a mythology about life in Tiger Bay, which is clearly of their own making, derived from a century of media misrepresentation. However, today they even come tagging ethnic credentials behind them, having gained experience in black ghetto areas in Britain. This form of stereotypical thinking is now added to the legend of Tiger Bay, being perceived as a black community — instead of the multi-racial and intra-cultural community that it has always been.

Reporters come from other regions in search of "The Black Community." Locals then have to assure them there isn't one here by declaring our multi-ethnic reality. Then we are accused of being black people who don't know or recognise our heritage. That, of course, is not the case, as I hope the reader will have realised by having read the pages of this book.

Media today bring us stories of "ethnic cleansing" in Bosnia. United Nations peace-keeping forces are undertaking armed invasions of Somalia. Yet, at the turn of this century, the community of Tiger Bay had already realised multi-ethnic community relations. We, in Tiger Bay, are a racially heterogeneous community, representative of an advanced form of social existence. The current emphasis on the Balkanisation of ethnic groups, throughout the world is the retrogressive form. The inhabitants of Tiger Bay witnessed the birth of the ethnically homogeneous communities of Brixton, St Pauls, Toxteth, etc. Tiger Bay society is the oldest continous multi-ethnic community in Britain [with the possible exception of Liverpool Eight] and, it must be emphasised, never was a black community. From the beginning, it was always a multi-racial and intra-cultural community. In Tiger Bay, there were no all-black schools or institutions. When community members point homeward to the lands of their ancestral forefathers, with feet firmly planted in Celtic soil, they point to Egypt, Yemen, Arabia, Somaliland, Sierra Leone, Nigeria, Malta, Cape Verde, Spain, etc., and needless to say the islands of the Caribbean. By the 1950s, Tiger Bay was a nation unto itself.

Will there be a Tiger Bay on the lake in the new Cardiff Bay? Well, despite the many setbacks suffered by this community, many remnants of the old Tiger Bay families remain. And it is through those families that perhaps our history will not disappear into oblivion.

In the minds of some, it has gone and good-riddance! In the minds of others, it is a sad demise. Yet, to me, it is here to stay. It is my home. A home that remains wherever I go. A home deep down in my heart. Submerged though it be in the new Cardiff Bay, this Tiger Bay shall continue to be and never be forgotten.

When I was young, people used to say, "In Tiger Bay you can see the world in one square mile." And, here today, we still live together, despite interference from well-intentioned interlopers, who do more harm than good for lack of realisation that Tiger Bay should be recognised as a successful example of urban village development for cities across Europe. Or, perhaps, it is only Merlin's magic that can provide the vital ingrediant for creating such intra-cultural harmony and, thus, it is only here, in this tiny square mile, in the land of the Dragon that the Tiger can roam in peace.

NOTES

Chapter Two

1 Fryer, Peter: *Staying Power: The History of Black People in Britain* (London, 1984) p. 308. The first quotation in the passage is from Neil Evans in "The South Wales Race Riots of 1919," *Llafur: Journal of the Society for the Study of Welsh Labour History*, vol. 3, no.1 (Spring 1980), pp. 5-29. The other quotes are from the *South Wales News*, 4th June 1919 and 7th June 1919.

Chapter Seven

2 Haddon, Alfred C: *The Races of Man and Their Distribution*, New York, MacMillan, 1925, pp. 24-25.

REFERENCES

Cardiff Bay Development Corporation, Richards, Sue in: *Education Resource Pack*, (1987).

Evans, Neil: "The South Wales Race Riots of 1919," *Llafur: The Journal of the Society for the Study of Welsh History*, III/1 (Spring 1980).

Fryer, Peter: *Staying Power, The History of Black People in Britain*, London and Sydney: Pluto Press, 1984.

Haddon, Alfred C: *The Races of Man and Their Distribution*, New York, MacMillan, 1925.

South Wales News, no. 14,651 (14 June 1919), 5;
No 14,562 (17 June 1919), 5.

Western Mail & South Wales Echo, July 7, 8, & 10, 1935.

THE TIGER BAY STORY

The Tiger Bay Story is the first book to
provide an insider's view of life in Old
Tiger Bay. Drawing on personal
memories, family history and interviews
with old-timers the book is an account of
an aspect of Welsh heritage that is all too
frequently overlooked. Humorous yet
serious, this is a book everyone will
enjoy. It is highly recommended for
readers of all ages.

Quoted from original cover

*"New book a certain hit. There have been a number of well-
written books about Cardiff's docklands, and now there is
one that goes right to the heart of the day-to-day life in
Tiger Bay ... The book is **The Tiger Bay Story** and the
author has dug deeply into the story seams of his neighbour-
hood, and enlivened his writing with splashes of humour..."*

Bill Barrett, Cardiff Post

Published & Distributed by
Dragon & Tiger Enterprises
199 Loudoun Square, Cardiff Bay
Cardiff, CF10 5JJ, South Wales
Tel: 029 2048 1129

About The Author

● ●

Neil Sinclair is a native son of the Tiger Bay community. Although he spent over two decades in the United States, this absence served only to intensify his interest in his roots. Particularly since his birthplace experienced a complete transformation during the early 1960s, his desire to record for posterity, to the best of his ability, the true essence of the life lived in his community is his life-long ambition.

He graduated with a Masters' Degree from the University of California at Los Angeles and gained his Bachelors' Degree from the same university at Berkeley.

Since his return to Cardiff at the beginning of the 1990s, he has written *The Tiger Bay Story* and *The Cardiff Bay Experience*. In addition he produced a video entitled *A Stroll Through Tiger Bay*, which was the culmination of a decade-long series of history walks. Negotiating with the Cardiff Bay Development Corporation to sponsor these walks, he was able to offer them to the general public free of charge. The Open University has also recorded his history walk and regularly airs this program on television.
More recently, 2003 saw the publication of his *Endangered Tiger - A Community Under Threat*.

As a recognized source of information on the life and times of the community of Tiger Bay, he is often seen in the media discussing his favourite subject.